CREATIVITY 1, 2, 3

Martha Cray-Andrews, Ph.D.
Susan Baum, Ph.D.

Illustrated by
Sharon Richman and Laura Jenkins Thompson

SECOND EDITION
Fifth Printing

Royal Fireworks Press

Unionville, New York

Copyright © 1996, R Fireworks Publishing Company, Ltd.
All Rights Reserved.

Originally published in 1992 by Trillium Press, Inc.

Royal Fireworks Press
First Avenue, PO Box 399
Unionville, NY 10988-0399
TEL: (845) 726-4444
FAX: (845) 726-3824
email: rfpress@frontiernet.net
ISBN: 0-89824--076-X

Printed in the United States of America using soy-based inks on acid-free recycled paper by the Royal Fireworks Printing Co. of Unionville, New York.

Contents

Part I: Theoretical Framework — 1
- Introduction — 2
- Are You Ready? — 5
- Is Your Room Ready? — 10

Part II: Creativity Training — 13
- Designing A Creativity Training Program — 14
- Teaching Fluency, Flexibility, Originality, Elaboration — 19

Part III: Classroom Applications — 23
- Integrating Creativity Into The Curriculum — 24
- Mathematics
  - Class Activities:
    - Number Hunt — 25
    - Simple Symmetry — 26
    - Graph-ol-ogy — 27
    - A World Without Circles — 28
    - Finders Keepers — 29
    - Dome Mania — 30
  - Independent Activities:
    - My Counting Book — 35
    - Hide and Seek — 37
    - Timing Around — 39
    - Fashion Designer — 41
    - Stump the Riddler — 43
    - Squares are Superior — 45
  - Buff Activities:
    - Games to Learn By — 47
    - Shopping Spree — 49
    - Travel Agency, Inc. — 51
    - Survey Specialist — 53
- Science
  - Class Activities:
    - Chickens Aren't the Only Ones — 56
    - Talking Without Words — 57
    - Staying Safe — 58
    - Grabbing Health — 59
    - To Float or Not to Float — 60
    - Science Snooper — 63
  - Independent Activities:
    - Name That Tune — 65
    - Spaced Out Planets — 67
    - Menu Madness — 69
    - Picture This — 71
    - The Play's the Thing — 73
    - I Spy — 75
  - Buff Activities:
    - Seasonal Stroll — 77
    - Ecology Watch — 79
    - Sliding In — 81
    - Cloudy Day — 83

- Social Studies
    - Class Activities:
        - Our History — 85
        - My History — 86
        - Special Studies — 87
        - Different or Same — 88
        - Family Mapping — 89
        - In Our Town — 90
    - Independent Activities:
        - Match Box Parade — 91
        - Favorite Days — 93
        - Toy Stories — 95
        - Guess Where — 97
        - Clothes Designer — 99
    - Buff Activities:
        - Your Town — 102
        - The Day You Were Born — 103
        - If My School Could Talk — 105
        - My Birthday Journal — 107
- Language Arts
    - Class Activities:
        - Center Stage — 109
        - The Mouse House — 110
        - Class Characters — 111
        - Just Like Me — 112
        - Letter Lovers — 113
        - Pass The Bag — 114
    - Independent Activities:
        - Photo Biography — 115
        - Artistic Readers — 117
        - To Pop or Not to Pop Book — 119
        - Mother Goose, Where are you? — 121
        - Mobile Mystery — 123
        - Mood Molding — 125
    - Buff Activities:
        - Talk of the Town — 127
        - Extra, Extra! Read all about it! — 129
        - Believe it or not! — 131
        - Pic Pick — 133
        - In My Family — 135

Part IV: Other Opportunities to Enhance Creativity — 137

Bibliography — 147

Part I

Theoretical Considerations

Creativity involves considering environment, personality, process and product.

Introduction

Have you ever watched young children at play and noticed how they use toys in different ways? They do not think of the intended purposes of the toys. They use them as props. A book is a tunnel for cars, or used to balance on heads, pile for steps, cut, color, or throw. Have you ever listened to a young child describe a physical phenomenon? "The sun is following me. It chases me wherever I go. Everywhere, look." "When my sister plays the piano, it sounds like the music is dancing all around." Have you ever come face to face with a young child's inventiveness when confronted with a "crime"? "I didn't draw on the wall. My friend Tickeroo did. I told him not to. I took his crayons away and pushed him out the window." The child is not only original but able to elaborate beautifully on a theme.

What happens to free interpretation of the environment as the child enters school? Experience contradicts original perceptions. For example: the sun is not moving. We move around the sun. Social pressure forces conformity. Brothers, sisters, and friends laugh at the absurdity of an imaginary friend. Criticism from the environment curtails originality. "Take that book off your head. Books are to read." Finally, the imaginative child enters school and perhaps encounters a classroom like this:

> The little boy went first day of school
>
> He got some crayons and started to draw
>
> He put colors all over the paper
>
> For colors are what he saw
>
> And the teacher said...What are you doing, young man?
>
> I'm painting flowers, he said.
>
> She said...It's not time for art, young man
>
> And anyway flowers are green and red
>
> There's a time for everything, young man
>
> And a way it should be done
>
> You've got to show concern for everyone else
>
> For you're not the only one.
>
> And she said...Flowers are red, young man
>
> Green leaves are green
>
> There's no way to see flowers any other way
>
> Than the way they always have been seen.
>
> written by Harry Chapin
> 1978 Elektra/Asylum Records

This is an extreme example of what might happen in school; however, we think it is a good starting point for discussing the creative process and why primary teachers should integrate creativity into their school programs. We must nourish the creative seed and watch it grow so we have silver bells and cockle shells but not all in a row.

Young children come to school with personality traits conducive to creativity. What happens along the way? In order to nourish creativity we must have a common understanding of what creativity is. According to Donald MacKinnon, creativity has four aspects: the product, the person, the process, and the situation.

Until school, a child's learning is primarily informal. Then, the school becomes the environment for most of the child's day. A more formal approach to learning occurs. Children must learn the rules of the classroom. They must learn the correct way to write their names, the correct way to fill in a worksheet. They must learn to follow directions in a group game. From an informal world of learning the children arrive in an atmosphere which requires one right answer, the single, correct way of doing things. There are so many rules and directions to follow that the child may no longer be comfortable in situations having little structure and no right answer.

Primary grade teachers have a triple responsibility. First, you must train the children to think convergently, to come to a common conclusion, to arrive at the right answer. After all, creative spelling is not acceptable. Second, you must provide opportunities for the children to think divergently, arriving at many different, unusual ideas. Finally, you must teach the children to understand the difference between the two types of thinking and when each is appropriate.

If we are to foster creativity, we must know some strategies that will help children develop skills in productive thinking. Thus, the main emphasis of this book: how to make creativity an integral part of the classroom.

A construct is helpful when we look at creativity and how to manage it in a classroom. The construct can help us organize, build, and evaluate. It can offer a hook on which to hang our ideas. It allows us to direct activities and expectations in a purposeful way without falling into the supermarket trap of buying one of everything on the shelf simply because it is there. It makes sense to look for a construct that takes into account the dimensions that define the classroom.

What form does the construct take? For us, three strands stand out: the environment, the student and the content. Through action, interaction, and reaction these three strands create the educational situation and bring learning to life. In order to show their interaction, it is important to understand each strand.

The first component, environment, deals with the setting and the strategies which help develop the creative process. What kind of environment encourages children to think creatively and to solve problems?

Strand two, the student, has two parts: the affective and the cognitive. Important to the affective area are the feelings that allow or prevent the student's response. A willingness to examine open-ended or unanswered problems, a readiness to take a chance, a comfort with not knowing, and a desire to investigate are all included in the affective domain. All children have the potential to act in these areas, but they may not act equally well in each. The ability to respond in a creative manner requires a person to do more than passively receive and restructure ideas. Creativity is an active process requiring involvement—a rising to the occasion. The affective domain relates to an emotional readiness to deal with unknowns, questions, and challenges.

The cognitive strand contains the intellectual areas that allow a person to play with ideas and to act creatively. The first step is for the student to become fluent. Fluency is the ability to go beyond the initial idea, to break away from the "one right answer" assumption, to go beyond the initial idea to many ideas for solutions. The next step requires the student to change the direction of thought and to offer solutions from different angles: flexibility. The third step is to develop originality. The child has moved from MANY answers to DIFFERENT answers and now the challenge is to develop NEW AND UNIQUE answers (the answers may be new and unique to the student, to most people of the same age, or to the world). The final step in this process is to elaborate on a possible solution, to move from the drawing board to the test site. The student must ADD DETAILS. Will the solution work?

The third strand, the content, is the subject matter, the curriculum. The curriculum alters creativity from the Friday afternoon fun-time activity to the arena of constant use. If we are going to emphasize creativity as an important process, we must allow it to play a part in the lives of the children—it must be allowed to have an outlet. The curriculum offers a platform for ideas and problems through which creativity can emerge. It brings the creative process and product from the training session to the field. Without this, creativity stands the chance of being just another add-on to an already full week.

The role of the teacher is an important one. You design an environment that encourages creative thinking, and you demonstrate the strategies that encourage fluency, flexibility, originality, and elaboration. Finally, you provide the platform—the curriculum—by which the children are able to take off in creative thinking.

Are You Ready?

Creativity in the classroom does not have to be threatening or an added burden; it can be fun, exciting, and rewarding to you. Creativity can be a mood in the room which livens every day. It can enhance curriculum, increase motivation, and enrich the environment. A classroom that fosters creativity is an exciting place to learn. It transforms the learning environment into a laboratory which encourages students to experiment with ideas and celebrate their fulfillment. You will find that the children will become more active in the learning process and enjoy it more. Confidence will develop as the children feel more and more comfortable testing their own ideas. Group dynamics will improve as the children share ideas with each other and gain respect for individual differences among themselves. They can work together improving ideas, gaining skill in looking at situations from many perspectives. You, too, will benefit because the children will share responsibility for the classroom. A variety of projects will begin to emerge, and if the children are truly involved, there will be less policing needed. You can become a learner and enjoy discovery with the children. The kinds of lessons learned will be relevant and applicable to everyday life. Most important, the children in the class will be motivated to learn.

Perhaps you are thinking, "I'm not creative, so how can I have a creative classroom? I can't think of those clever ideas." If so, you have fallen prey to the "It looks good on paper syndrome." You are not alone. Many teachers will agree that benefits do exist in having a creative classroom but feel totally inadequate in providing such an environment. They are plagued with concerns such as "I'm not creative," "Where do I begin?," "Are the children ready for this?," and "Am I ready for this?" It is important to look at some of these concerns before moving from paper to practice.

The following is a quick checklist to help you look at some of your personal feelings about creativity in the classroom. Read each of the statements and check whether you agree or disagree. This is not a test, but move through the list quickly, checking your first reaction.

		AGREE	DON'T AGREE
1.	You have to be creative yourself to foster it in children.	_____	_____
2.	Learning is not fun.	_____	_____
3.	All children need drill.	_____	_____
4.	The teacher must be in control of what is to be learned and how it is to be learned.	_____	_____
5.	All objectives must be specific.	_____	_____
6.	The basics must be mastered before frills are added to the school day.	_____	_____
7.	A quiet environment is necessary for learning to take place.	_____	_____
8.	To make creativity an integral part of the school day, you must change your whole style of teaching.	_____	_____

If you checked "Don't Agree" seven or eight times:
   You probably have an exciting classroom and are fostering creativity already. The rest of this handbook should serve to add some structure to the process and may suggest ideas for encouraging creativity.

If you checked "Don't Agree" four, five, or six times:
   You may need some support to let you know you can make your classroom a more creative place. The remainder of this book should give you that pat on the back and provide you with practical suggestions for application.

If you checked "Don't Agree" one, two, or three times:
   Don't panic. You too can have a creative classroom. The rest of this book should help you recognize the benefits of creativity in the classroom and provide you with a beginning.

1. You have to be creative yourself to foster it in children.

You are probably more creative than you think you are. Remember the four ingredients to creativity? Fluency, flexibility, originality, and elaboration are processes. You probably practice these skills every day as you encounter problems.

Example: You have unexpected company for dinner. What do you serve them? You quickly brainstorm for options:

- Call out for pizza.
- Throw all your cold cuts in a salad and call if "Chef's Delight."
- Search the cookbook.
- Proclaim a personal fast day.
- Sauté all your frozen left-overs and throw them over spaghetti.

Example: You have had theatre tickets for six months, but the night of the performance your car breaks down. How do you get to the theatre?

- Call a friend.
- Hitch-hike.
- Take a bus.
- Rent a car.
- Ride your lawn mower.

In these cases you are problem solving. Perhaps you have never looked at teaching as problem solving. To add your creativity to the lesson, choose one activity and change it in some way. Instead of giving a worksheet asking the children to identify the number in various sets, ask them to construct three dimensional sets and identify their construction by numerals. Consider the assignment of a monthly book report. In addition to the one page summary, offer options of creating a diorama, a mobile, a play, a review, a cartoon strip, a puppet show. All of these options answer the purpose of checking comprehension.

2. Learning is not fun.

Some people feel learning should be hard work, and hard work cannot be fun. To enjoy hard work is a contradiction. For children, play is fun. Remember that enjoyment is not an indication of the difficulty of the task but a factor which may help the children stick with the task once started. Think of your own learning experiences. Do you remember one you hated? Contrast that with an experience you enjoyed. What were the differences in the way they were taught? Did you have a more active involvement in the pleasant experience? Most people find that to be a major difference.

3. All children need drill.

Remember the purpose of drill. We want the children to practice a given skill or process. Does it have to be done in a repetitive manner? Consider the language arts objective of developing sequencing skills. A typical assignment in a language arts workbook is to read a paragraph or two and then number the events in a list given below the story. Instead of drilling the skill of sequencing as the workbook offers, add a creative dimension of your own. Have the children write, tape or tell a story with the events out of order. This activity taps the processes of flexibility, originality, and elaboration. The children would have to understand sequencing to do the task.

4. The teacher must be in control of what is to be learned and how it is to be learned.

Learning cannot be controlled; it happens continuously. Teachers may decide what they will teach, but it is doubtful they can control what is learned. As children observe, they learn patterns, formulate ideas, and arrive at solutions other than those stated in the curriculum. Let them have a time and a space to test their ideas and solutions. A first grader in charge of watering the plants for the week may notice the leaves turn toward the sun. Your problem is that photosynthesis and plants are a spring science unit. What do you do? Letting the child have time to research the problem will give you an "expert" in the spring. A possible peer teaching situation has been created by letting the child take control of the topic to be studied.

5. All objectives must be specific.

Many objectives can be specific, but there is a danger of not being able to see the forest for the trees. We can become so concerned about the pieces of learning that we miss the big ideas as they pass through the room. If there is a general goal such as self expression or creative growth, it may be beneficial to alter a specific objective to let the child pursue the idea or project that has captured interest. Forcing all the children's ideas to the position of add-on will not encourage the growth you are after. There are times when it is more appropriate to have a child work on a new idea instead of the workbook rather than in addition to the workbook.

6. The basics must be mastered before frills are added to the school day.

We may be back to the forest and the trees analogy. The basics of reading, writing, mathematics, social studies, and science do not have to be taught in a repetitive manner. By integrating creativity training and problem-solving activities in the curriculum areas, the children will become more involved in their learning and be better able to transfer their learning to everyday experience.

7. A quiet environment is necessary for learning to take place.

Noise can exist in positive ways. Brainstorming, delight in discovery, sharing ideas, and teaching all require noise. Don't be afraid of it—just learn how to control the volume.

8. To make creativity an integral part of the school day, you must change your whole style of teaching.

Any change that you want to last must occur at a pace that is comfortable for the people involved. That includes you and the children. If creativity training and creativity in the classroom are new ventures, begin slowly with direction from the children. You must be able to answer these three questions: "Why am I making this change?," "How am I going to make this change?," and "Am I comfortable with this change?" As a beginning, give a bulletin board to the children. Allow them planning time and materials to take charge of its content. Allow an assignment in a curriculum area to be designed by the children. Give one planned period each week to a child's spontaneous idea.

If you are able to accomplish some of these ideas, you will begin to feel more comfortable with creativity in your classroom. The children will become more involved in their learning, and the cycle will be underway.

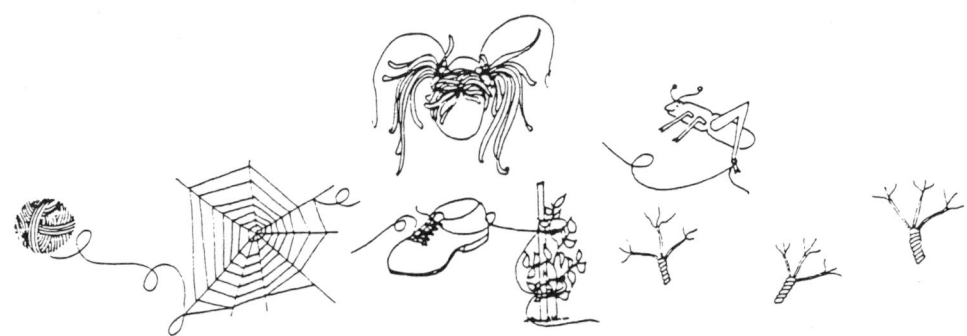

Is Your Room Ready?

As we stated earlier, the teacher must understand the kind of environment that encourages creative thinking and problem solving. What is that environment?

We are talking about an atmosphere of acceptance. Acceptance does not mean anything a child says or does must be accepted. It is, however, a recognition that the affective parts of creativity need an environment supportive of risk taking. The expectation of "one right answer" must be thrown away. Discarding this expectation requires a clear signal so the children learn that certain questions, activities, and discussions are investigative or problem-solving. The children must switch from convergent (one answer) to divergent (many answers) thinking. Signalling this transition will help them recognize the switch. Acceptance of a time out or incubation period is also necessary. We must recognize that all children will not work, think, or act within the same time frame. There needs to be an option for time out to think about the problem or idea. Allowing time out will lead the children to choose different ways to find or solve a problem. To the casual observer it will appear that the children are involved in very different things.

As an example, let's suppose the children were given the problem of designing an egg carrier for a single egg. The egg carrier had to provide enough protection so it could be dropped from a height of fifteen feet onto pavement and the uncooked egg would remain whole. Some children would begin construction immediately. Others would begin sketching carrier designs. Some would start looking through books or talking with friends to gather ideas. Still others would work on some unrelated activity but be thinking of ideas. If the teacher put a one hour time limit on finding a solution, it's easy to see that the first two groups mentioned have a chance of developing an egg carrier as long as materials are available. However, the time restriction puts the last two groups at a definite disadvantage. In order to allow an incubation period, arrange the trial time for the next day or the next week. It offers more children an opportunity to become involved.

There is also a place for plain old mucking about. In real life problem solving, solutions are frequently arrived at in a round-about fashion. We consider ourselves lucky if solutions come quickly and efficiently. Yet, in the classroom we often require the students to find a quick, appropriate solution. Mucking about is the try, try again activity that goes on when solutions are being sought. It leads to the restructuring and adaptation that improves the first idea. The child begins to work with materials, and an idea forms. He or she sees certain changes would make it better so the improved idea begins to take shape. Initially, the child might not have known what the project would be. It evolves as the child works with the materials. Remember the egg carrier problem? Josh was at home working on the problem. He found a Leggs egg. He spent some time mucking about with the Leggs egg. He filled it with various things and decided he wanted some shock absorbing substance to surround the egg that would be housed in the Leggs egg. What was the problem? It kept dripping. Completely filling the Leggs egg was impossible. He wanted something that would solidify. Jello. He filled the halves of the Leggs egg with Jello. It solidified. He carved a hole for the egg. It worked. Josh's mucking about led to solving the problem.

All the variables we've listed (acceptance, signalling, incubation, and mucking about) refer to creating a laboratory environment for children. In a laboratory, we expect that ideas will be pursued and tested. As adults, we choose a variety of ways to check our ideas. We read, try the idea out, think about it, discuss it with others. In this environment, children have these same options open to them. They do not work in isolation.

However, merely arriving at a solution is not sufficient. The solution must be tried. Testing leads to the elaboration and adaptation that is so important in the creative process. The children move from the role of passive thinkers to the role of active experimenters. Along the way, they will learn that initial ideas do not always work. There will be times when several ideas will be tested before a workable solution appears. This testing and re-testing encourages sustained effort in pursuit of a goal. We often speak of the need for children to develop abilities to stay with a problem to its successful completion. Yet, we do little to create an environment where this is expected or even allowed.

If we are going to encourage idea testing, we must prepare for the times a child finds a dead end. The idea being pursued shows no promise. This is accepted. If we are truly encouraging children to be creative in their thinking and problem solving, there is no safe way to channel each idea or solution to a successful finish. It becomes your role to show supportive recognition of effort, and to help with the reality that some ideas do not work. In a laboratory setting, a dead end does not necessarily signal an end. It may mean re-evaluation and a new start.

The area of evaluation is important to the creative process. In the laboratory, evaluation means joint effort. A new idea or solution may not be recognized by a child. Very often you will have to

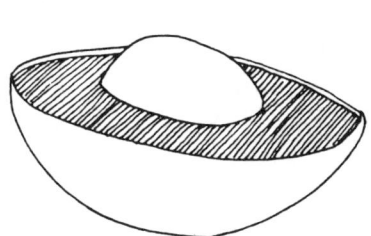 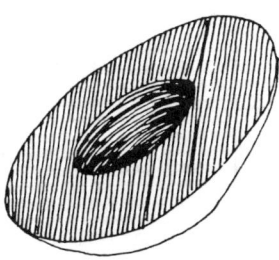

discuss the accomplishment with the child. Both of you need to look at the idea or project to determine its good and bad points. But to rely on your evaluation alone may encourage a dependency leading the child to others for evaluation rather than self-evaluating. The child should learn that evaluation is a process of setting standards and judging according to those standards.

Referring again to the egg carrier problem, several standards were determined by the children participating in the project. Their standards were: accessibility of materials, size of carrier, cost of materials, time to construct, and successful landing. Several entries received high marks in one or two categories but low marks in others. Josh's carrier, the Leggs egg, scored highly in all categories. The important point is that the children designed standards appropriate to the situation and judged by using those standards. This kind of discussion and evaluation encourages acceptance of varied approaches to a problem. The children are learning that a cursory look is not an appropriate evaluation.

A final step in creating an environment which encourages creativity is the consideration of audience. To build on sustained effort, the unique idea or solution must be allowed to have impact. The child must be allowed to share the idea or solution with an interested group of people. This differs from a stand-up-in-class-and-report activity. In this case the audience chooses to be there. You encourage the child to share the idea or project with a group of people who share the child's interest. This can be accomplished by scheduling a forum time when children have the option of signing up to hear a forum speaker. We have scheduled such forums in parts of the classroom, in the library, on the playground, or anyplace a group of children can gather to talk about a chosen topic. Fore some children a display of their project is more acceptable. Still others enjoy taking their projects outside of the school, bringing them to the group that can act on them: the town officers, historical society, or newspaper. Whatever the audience, in each case it is a self-selected group of people who share an interest with the child.

This kind of involvement takes time. But remember that we have been talking about opportunities for creativity, not mandated novelty. All children will not pursue an idea to its conclusion every time. In the egg carrier problem forty-seven children had the opportunity to become involved. At the test site eleven children presented egg carriers. Remember too that we are encouraging you to use curriculum content as the point of departure for creativity. If the curriculum is used, many of the ideas and projects will parallel the activities going on in the classroom.

🐤	ACCESSIBILITY OF MATERIALS	SIZE	$	🕐	SUCCESSFUL LANDING
JOSH	○	○	○	○	○
ALI	○	🥚	🥚💥	○	🥚
LESLIE	🥚	○	🥚💥	🥚💥	🥚💥

Part II

Creativity Training

Yes, research confirms that everyone can be taught to become more creative.

Designing A Creativity Training Program

In this section we distinguish between the teacher as a trainer and the teacher as a designer. As trainer, you will organize lessons in creativity. These sessions allow children the time to look at some of the skills involved in creativity. The most common error in implementing creativity in the classroom relates to training. Some people assume three half-hour sessions each week are sufficient to make all children creative. This assumption parallels the spelling program dilemma.

When we were children, every student in our school had a spelling book. Every day there was a fifteen to thirty minute period for us to do our spelling. These time periods were our spelling training sessions. We were supposed to be learning the skills that would make us able spellers or, failing that, at least memorizing the words for that week's test. Most teachers would not argue against training for spelling. But many teachers make the assumption that the Friday test identifies the able spellers. How many of Friday's able spellers could still spell on Monday? How many would even try to spell on Monday? To be an able speller implies more than a once-a-week peak experience of putting letters in correct order. This dilemma exists in creativity training, too. There is a need for training sessions. The children need to develop skills and strategies that will help them become more creative. They also need to be encouraged, expected, and allowed to use the skills and strategies at times other than the creativity training sessions.

• Divergent Thinking Skills •

The main areas in creativity training are **FLUENCY, FLEXIBILITY, ORIGINALITY, AND ELABORATION**. Many of the published materials in creativity training structure the lessons on these four skills. Having published materials available can be an asset in getting a training program started, but you can begin without them. The first step is to make the time schedule for the training. If you do not make the conscious effort to assign time slots to creativity training, one hundred and six reasons will surface to push the training off day after day after day. The schedule established, the next step is to plan the activities. It is possible to use the four categories (fluency, flexibility, originality, and elaboration) as the steps in the program. Choosing activities that illustrate the four categories and talking about the creative process will help the children use the strategies in problem-solving situations.

Brainstorming For Fluency

Activities that develop fluency ask the children to think of many options. You may ask the children to think of as many uses for a rock as they can. You may ask for as many uses for a shoe, a string, or a newspaper. The key word is "many." Usually, this activity is done verbally in groups. Some person, usually you, acts as recorder so the group's ideas can be written. This group process is called brainstorming. The rules are: any person may participate, no praise or criticism is given for any response, and the piggy-backing (getting an idea from someone else's idea) is allowed. In time, the children will be able to develop longer and longer lists to these fluency building questions. The children should be told the purpose of the activities. They need to know why they are doing these activities so they can make use of them in parallel situations. Children learn that brainstorming is a useful strategy for generating options. Through experience with brainstorming they will notice that the unusual ideas are not the first ideas. They will learn that thinking of more than one idea is possible and can lead to unusual ideas or solutions.

Flexibility

To illustrate flexibility, use the lists the brainstorming sessions generated. Let the children categorize the ideas. For example, using the answers offered to the question, "How many ways can you use a rock?," the categories might be a hitting object, a building object, a toy, or a game. The actual responses will suggest additional categories. The children can decide in which category each response fits. Looking at a variety of categories will help the children learn that ideas can come from different directions. The key word for flexibility is "different." The child who can think of sixteen uses for a rock may be considered fluent, but if each of the ideas shows the rock being used in construction, the child needs to work on becoming more flexible.

Originality

The next step is to develop originality. Using the brainstorming data again, look at the responses and have the children find the unusual ideas. What makes an idea unusual? The children will begin to recognize that looking at an idea differently from others, putting things together in ways that others do not go together makes an original idea. They will learn that original ideas are not often the first ideas on the list.

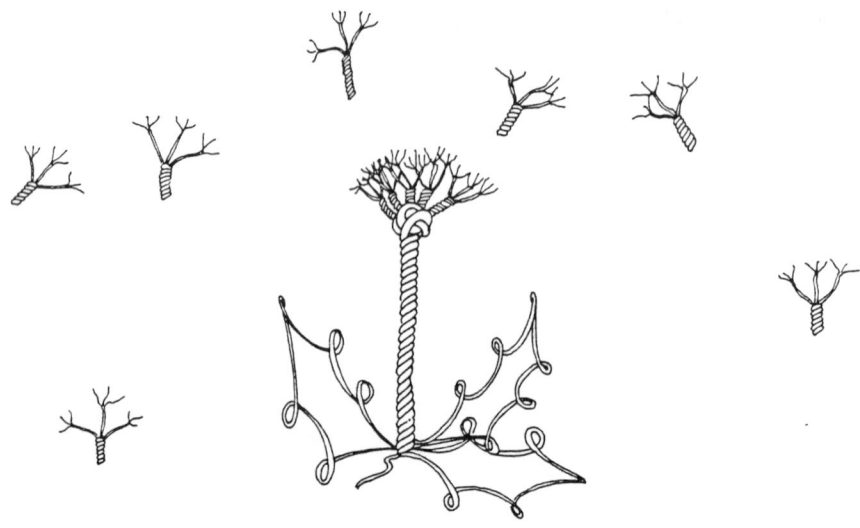

Elaboration

Finally, the children will work on elaboration. At this step they choose an idea to develop, and they add details to the idea so that it will work. For example, a child might choose to work with the idea of sculpting as a use for rocks. He or she would elaborate on this idea by telling how the rocks could be used for sculpting or by actually doing it. At this point, the child tests the idea to decide if it is possible. Will it work?

These four steps build an awareness of problem-solving strategies. The children will be able to go through the process on their own if you take care to discuss the "why" of the training as well as the "what." As the children improve in the four processes, the problems offered in the training sessions can change from "How many uses for a string?" to "How many ways can you think of to stop fighting on the playground?" The question can reflect a real problem for the children. After brainstorming, categorizing, finding unusual solutions, and developing the promising solutions, one or two might actually be tried. Using real problems in the training sessions will help the children transfer their abilities in creativity training exercises to creative problem solving in real life.

You can use picture books to introduce your students to the ideas of fluency, flexibility, originality, and elaboration. The selections listed below are outstanding examples of these concepts and in addition serve as models for books children can develop themselves. The books illustrating fluency give lots of ideas along a theme. Those indicative of flexibility show different ways of looking at things. The selections for originality demonstrate excellent uses for imagination and imagery. Last, the choices listed for elaboration exemplify how to add details to an idea.

Fluency

Demi. (1981). *Where is Willie Worm?* NY: Random House.

Silverstein, S. (1983). *Does Anybody Want To Buy A Cheap Rhinoceros?* NY: Macmillan.

Martin, Jr., B & Archambault, J. (1988). *Listen To The Rain.* NY: Henry Holt & Co.

Mason, L. (1989). *A Book Of Boxes.* NY: Simon & Shuster.

Flexibility

Lobel, A. (1988) *The Turnabout Wind.* NY: Harper & Row.

Clement, C. (1986). *The Painter And The Wild Swans.* NY: Dial Books.

Reid, M. (1990). *The Button Box.* NY: Dutton.

Wood, A. (1982). *Quick As A Cricket.* Singapore: Child's Play (International) Ltd.

Originality

Van Alsburg, C. (1984). *The Adventures Of Harris Burdick.* Boston: Houghton Mifflin. (All Van Alsburg books illustrate originality.)

Fleischam, P. (1988). *Rondo In C.* NY: Harper & Row.

Brighton, C. (1985). *The Picture.* London: Faber & Faber Ltd.

Mayhew, J. (1989). *Katie's Picture Show.* NY: Bantam Books.

Elaboration

Lobel, A. (1984). *The Rose In My Garden.* NY: Greenwillow.

Ryder, J. (1989). *Where Butterflies Grow.* NY: Dutton.

Radin, R. (1989). *High In The Mountains.* NY: MacMillan.

Siebert, D. (1988). *Mojave.* NY: Thomas Y. Crowell.

Teaching Fluency, Flexibility, Originality and Elaboration.

The following activities can be used to teach divergent thinking skills to your students. Make sure you define the terms so that they can apply the strategies to other situations. It is a good idea to hang a poster in your room with these terms defined.

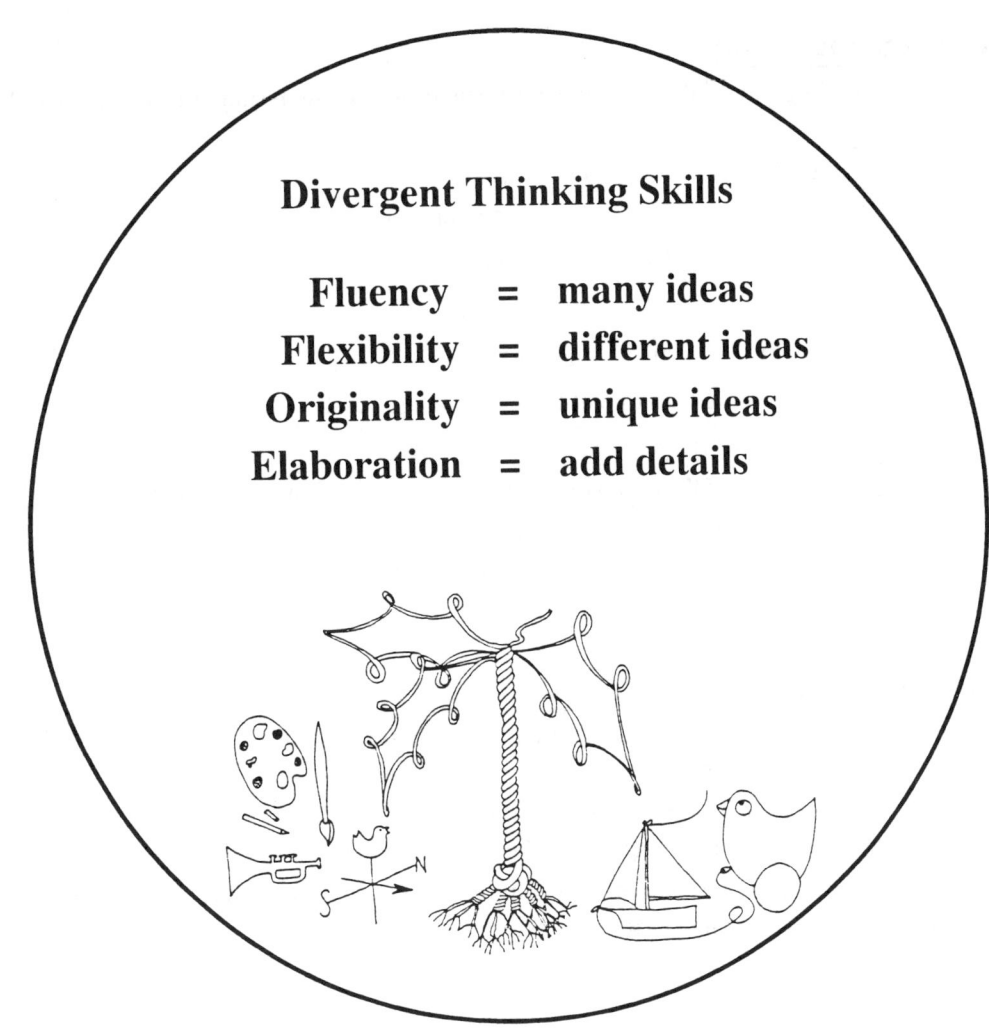

Divergent Thinking Skills

Fluency	=	many ideas
Flexibility	=	different ideas
Originality	=	unique ideas
Elaboration	=	add details

To focus on Fluency, ask the children:
1. How many ways can you use a chair?
2. What can you use a pumpkin seed for?
3. How many writing implements can you think of?
4. How many uses can you think of for a pan?
5. How many ways can you think of to say "5"?

(Be sure to keep these brainstorm lists for other activities!)

To encourage Flexibility:
1. Ask the children to think of items that fit categories. Give 3 categories for them to think about. Try:

animal	vegetable	toy
container	tool	weapon
slippery	dry	cold
blue	red	round
square	tall	heavy

(Some items will fit in more than one of the three categories!)

2. Using data from one of the brainstorming sessions, create categories, and ask the children to categorize the listed ideas.
3. Ask the children to find examples of "squares" in the environment.

To develop Originality:
1. Give each child seven pieces of colored construction paper (2" x 2" squares). Ask each child to think of a design/pattern that no one else will think of.
2. Using data from one of the brainstorming activities, ask the children to find the most unusual response(s). Discuss what makes them unusual (least frequent response).
3. Using the lists from the categorizing activities, ask the children to find the most unusual one(s). Discuss what makes them unusual.

To foster Elaboration:
1. Create a new character for a cartoon—giving picture, name, locale, and main characteristics.
2. Design a toy for a young child.

The following is a mini unit to be used with very young children
when teaching them divergent thinking skills.

Button Barrage

Day 1

Objective: To give children practice in brainstorming. To give children opportunities to be fluent — give many responses.

Procedure:

Warm-up: Children sit in a circle on the floor. Teacher asks, "Where have you ever seen a button?" Responses will probably begin with the category of buttons on clothing. They should expand to categories such as buttons on TV, "pop buttons," buttons as facial features of stuffed animals.

The teacher should set a number of responses she thinks the children should handle. ("Can we think of 20 ideas?")

Activity: Materials, magic markers, buttons and construction paper. Give children a large button to paste on a piece of construction paper. Have children think of a picture to draw around the button. Brainstorm ideas. Have children draw their own idea. Save picture for next lesson.

Day 2

Objective: To give opportunities for categorization skills. To "discover" what originality is.

Procedure:

Warm-up: The children sit in a circle on the floor. The teacher places red, yellow, and blue circles, squares, and triangles in the center. The children sort them in terms of color, size or shape. There should be a discussion of categorizing by attributes.

Activity: The teacher tells the class that they will categorize their button pictures. The categories may include flowers, buttons on clothing, on and off buttons, etc. Place the pictures on a bulletin board in categories.

The teacher leads children to see that the category with the smallest number of pictures will be the most original for that group — because not too many thought of the idea. Take care to point out that "most original" does not mean "best."

21

Day 3

Objective: To develop skill in using flexibility in their response.

Procedure: Divide children into three groups. Give each group a box of buttons. Tell them during their free play period they are to use the buttons in their activity. (Could be used as money, tokens in a game, food, making a trail, etc.) Have each group tell how they used their buttons. Be sure to compliment the children on their flexibility or their new use for buttons.

Day 4

Objective: To develop the skill of elaboration. To provide opportunities in creative movement and oral expression.

Procedure: Begin a story with the class. "One day, as I was walking down the street, my button jumped off my jacket. It said to me…." Have the children take turns at being the button and telling their part of the story. Their explanation should be taped to be listened to later.

After listening to the story, explain to the children that each child helped to elaborate on the story. The story was filled with lots of details because they all added something to it.

Part III

Curricular Applications

Creativity cannot thrive in a vacuum.

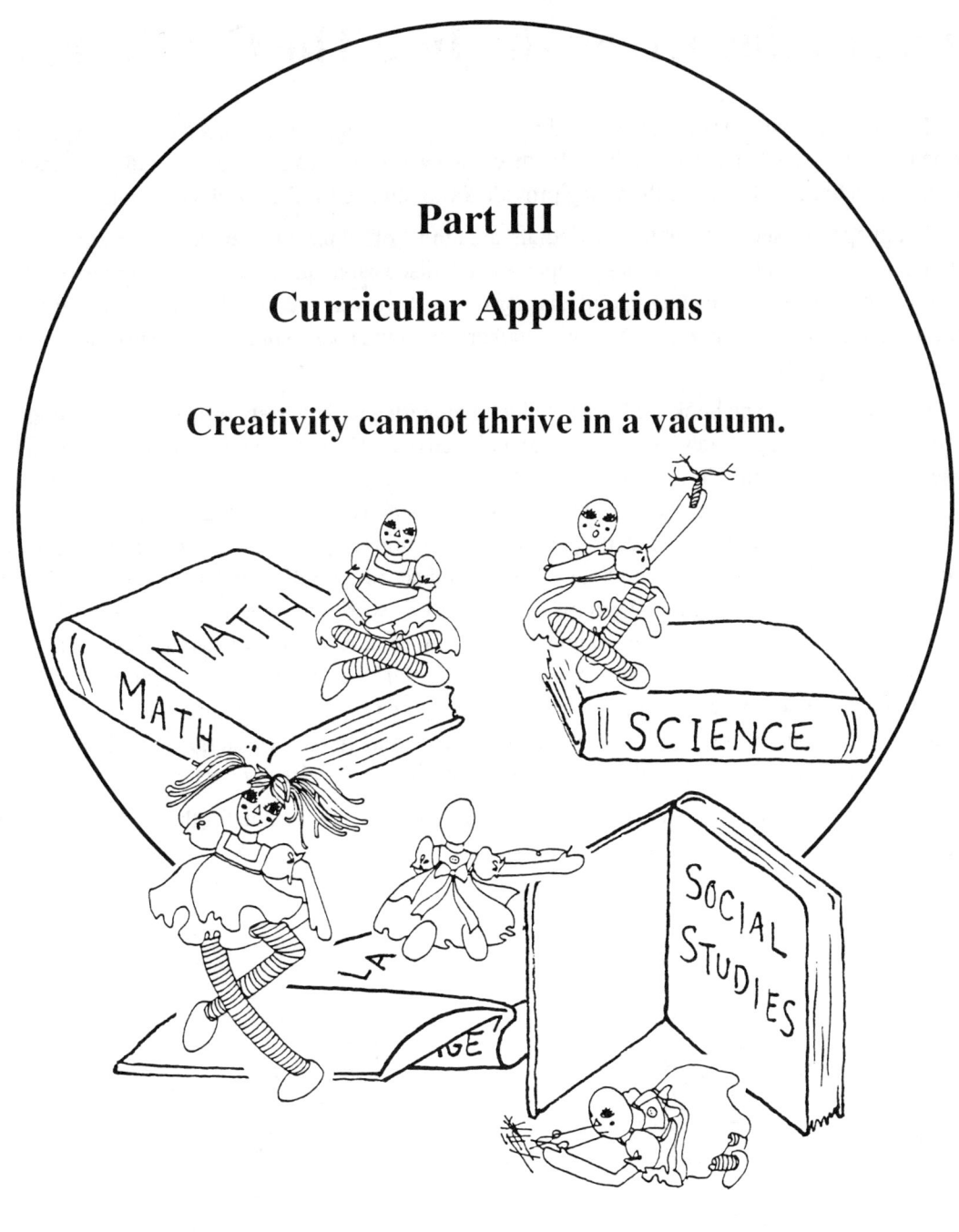

Integrating Creativity Into The Curriculum

In addition to periods of time devoted to creativity training, children need to have experiences during the school day to use these skills. We discussed ways the creative process could be integrated into the curriculum. The curriculum may provide a framework for the child's creativity.

Language arts seems to be the curriculum area most often used to develop creativity. We ask children to write poems and stories. Open-ended discussion questions encouraging divergent thinking are included in reading group discussions. However, we should not restrict divergent thinking activities to language arts. Science, mathematics, and social studies can be used to reinforce creative thinking, also.

In this section of the book we have provided you with a wide variety of learning activities that infuse creative thinking strategies into curricular objectives. We have divided the activities into four curricular areas: mathematics, science, social studies and language arts. There are three basic types of activities included in each section. The first set, class activities, are whole class lessons. They incorporate both a basic skills objective and a creative thinking objective. The teacher leads the lesson and provides guidance throughout. The second set of activities, independent activities, are designed so that individual or small groups of students can work on them independently. The third level designated for the "buff," are designed for the more able students in your class. These are students who have the need for a more advanced curriculum. The activities are not intended to be completed independently. Assistance from an adult may be necessary. The projects tend to be long term and involve creative productivity within the content area. In fact, we suggest using them in lieu of other assign,ents reinforcing skills that the "buff" probably has already mastered.

Notice that the independent activities and "buff" activities are written for the student. Feel free to cut out these pages, laminate them and use in centers.

MATHEMATICS
Class Activity

Number Hunt

Math Objective: application of number systems
Creativity Objective: fluency, flexibility
Materials Needed: recording book, pencil

Activity:
Have students record as many different ways numbers are used as they know. The ideas must come from what they see or hear, e.g., gallons at the gas station, money at a store, telephone numbers, scores as games. Keep a class list to see how many ways people use numbers. This could be added to the morning meeting activities to keep children looking and thinking about number use.

Extension:
Make a big book of all the ways people use numbers.

MATHEMATICS
Class Activity

Simple Symmetry

Math Objective: understanding of symmetry and balance
Creativity Objective: fluency
Materials Needed: tracing paper, drawing paper, scissors, pencils or markers, magazines

Activity:

After demonstrating the properties of symmetry, have each child find four examples of symmetry. Trace, draw, or cut out pictures in magazines of symmetrical objects. Make a collage of symmetrical things.

Extension:

Have students work with a variety of pictures to find the line of symmetry by tracing symmetrical objects and folding the tracing until the sides match up. If the lines do match up, the crease is the line of symmetry for that object. Some objects have no line of symmetry. Some have more than one. Let the children explore this pattern.

26

MATHEMATICS
Class Activity

Graph-ol-ogy

Math Objective: recognition of various types of graphs, creation of a bar graph

Creativity Objective: flexibility

Materials Needed: newspapers, business magazines, weekly news magazines, large index cards, glue, scissors

Activity:

Have the students cut out examples of graphs from the print materials. They can glue them on the index cards to keep them from tearing.

Have the students group the graphs into clusters that make sense to them. Discuss the categories. Complete the activity by using their examples to point out the different kinds of graphs: circle, line, bar, pictograph.

Extension:

Using a bar graph, graph the number of bar graphs, line graphs, circle graphs and pictographs in the class's collection.

MATHEMATICS
Class Activity

A World Without Circles

Math Objective: recognition of shapes in the environment, geometry

Creativity Objective: flexibility, elaboration

Materials Needed: mural paper, markers, paints, magazine pictures of scenes, e.g. rooms; gardens; houses; animals; magnifying glasses

Activity:

Divide the class into groups of 4 or 5 and have each group select a magazine picture with which to work. Have the children study their pictures. Ask them to find all the circles hidden in their pictures. A magnifying glass helps them take a close look.

Have the children imagine they lived in a world without circles. Have them make their own version of the magazine picture as it would look in a "circle-less" world. Share and discuss their ideas.

Extension:

Go on a shape hunt. Go on a safari around the school keeping track of the shapes encountered along the way such as square tiles (the group in charge of squares tallies these), rectangular windows, circular doorknobs. Graph the group's tallies.

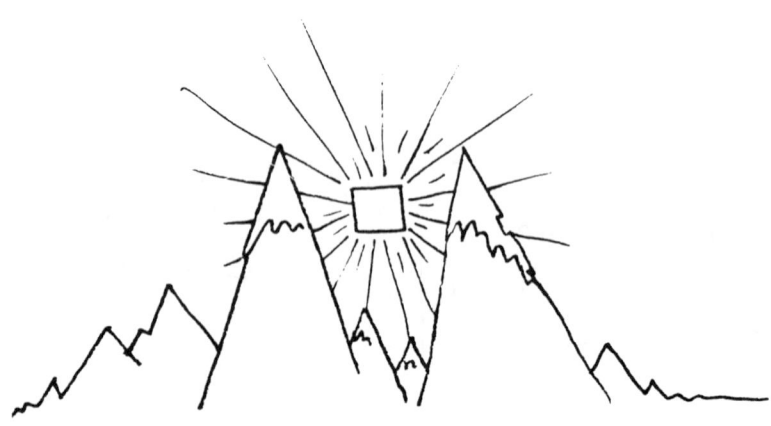

MATHEMATICS
Class Activity

Finders Keepers

Math Objective: graphing
Creativity Objective: fluency, flexibility, originality
Materials Needed: graph paper, markers, tally sheet, class list, copies of the "treasure hunt"

Treasure Hunt:

1. The number of children with brown hair.
2. The number of children with 3 or more brothers and sisters.
3. The number of children with a dog.
4. The number of children with a cat.
5. How many window panes in the room?
6. How many plants in the room?
7. How many children like video games?
8. How many children took a bus this morning?
9. How many children does your teacher have?
10. How many children are wearing shoes with laces?

Activity:

Divide the class into teams of five. Give each student a class list, a tally sheet and the treasure hunt questions. Tell them they have one week to gather the information. The teams should meet to decide how they will collect the information.

On day five, the teams will come together to report their results. The teacher will help them compile the data onto a bar graph. Discuss with them the two questions which are likely to vary from day to day (#8, 10). Did groups find different answers to those questions?

Extension:

Each team could pick four questions from the list and create an original pictograph which shows the responses in a unique way.

MATHEMATICS
Class Activity

Dome Mania

Math Objective: geometry - The triangle is a strong shape and used in creating many architectural structures.

Creativity Objective: originality, elaboration

Materials Needed: 60 toothpicks and 26 mini-marshmallows for each dome

Activity:

Lead children in constructing a geodesic dome (dome made from triangles; see next page for directions). To give children an idea of what the dome will look like, have them recall monkey bars or jungle gyms that are dome-shaped.

Then, give a copy of the directions to each student and help them with each step. The dome is built flat. Parts will pop up as toothpicks are joined. However, not until the <u>last</u> step does the structure take the shape of a dome.

After the dome is completed, let the class decide what their dome will be. Brainstorm possibilities; graph by categories; choose most original or individual favorites. If, for instance, the child wants the dome to be a hat, give him or her feathers or other materials to elaborate or decorate the idea.

Extension:

Let the dome be the basis for a class-chosen unit such as a future city, an eskimo village, or the ideal playground.

HOW TO CONSTRUCT A GEODESIC DOME
by Shirl Kaplan

1. Take 1 marshmallow and 5 toothpicks.

2. Put marshmallow on end of each toothpick.

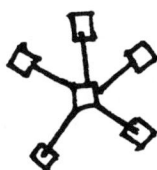

3. Connect each marshmallow with toothpicks.

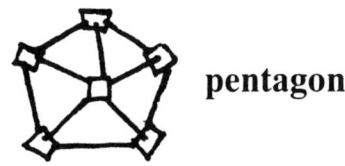

pentagon

4. Add 3 toothpicks to each marshmallow.

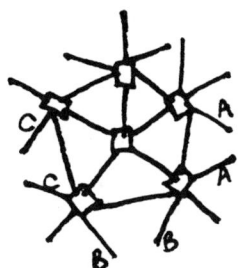

5. Join the toothpicks. (Attach "neighboring" picks with one marshmallow.)

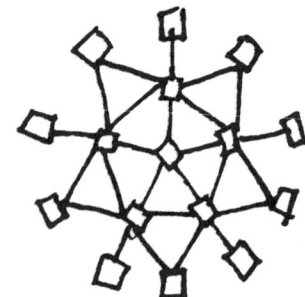

Attach:
A with A,
B with B, etc.

5-pointed star

6. Put marshmallow on single toothpick.

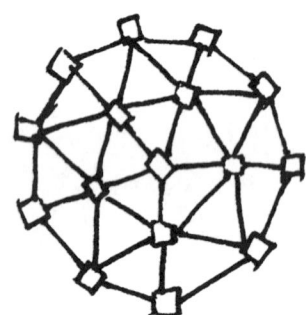

7. Connect all marshmallows with toothpicks.

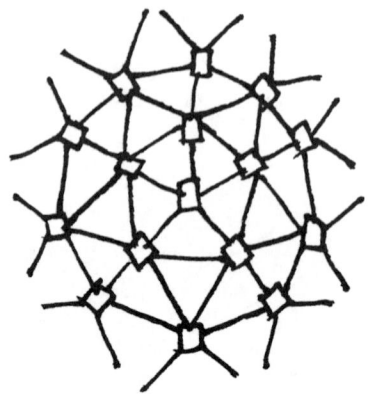

decagon

8. Add 2 toothpicks to each marshmallow.

32

9. Connect toothpicks (neighboring picks "hold hands").

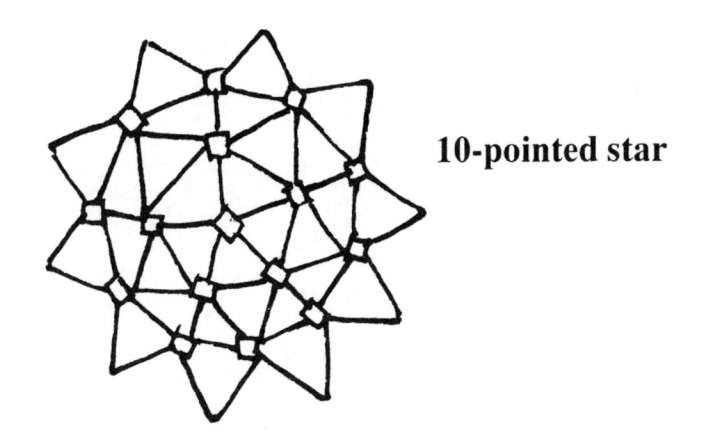

10-pointed star

10. Connect all marshmallows with toothpicks to form a GEODESIC DOME. It is at this point that the dome takes shape. Up until now, it is basically <u>flat.</u>

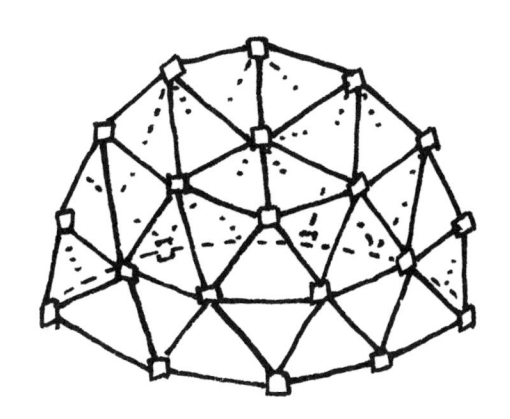

MATHEMATICS
Independent Activity

My Counting Book

You will get better at seeing number patterns and showing them in creative ways.
You will need: magazines, markers, construction paper, scissors, paste

Activity:

Make a counting book from 1 to 10 for a young child. First choose a theme like animals, transportation, people, space or ocean. Look for pictures or draw your own that go with your theme. Remember to find a new example for each new number. You may try using rhymes on each page.

For example, if you picked the ocean as your theme, your first four pages might look like this:

1 is for a great big wave that pushed me down.

2 is for shells I found on the ground.

3 is for umbrellas on the beach.

4 is for fishes just out of reach.

Try to make something unusual to make your numbers. When you have finished, make a cover for your book. Give it a title, and be sure to include the author's name. If you have a publishing house at your school, have your book bound.

Tips:

Brainstorming gives lots of ideas for the themes or examples of your themes.

How did I do?

	Yes	No
I thought of a good theme.	___	___
I thought of a different example for each page.	___	___
Each page goes with my theme.	___	___
I read my book to a young child.	___	___
Little children like my book.	___	___

MATHEMATICS
Independent Activity

Hide and Seek

You will get better at writing clues, drawing maps and using math facts.

You will need paper, pencils and a treasure to hide. The treasure could be something to eat, a picture you made or a prize from the teacher.

Activity:

You will hide the treasure somewhere in the classroom or playground and make a math puzzle treasure map so others can seek the prize. To make the map follow these steps:

1. Make a map of the room or playground.

2. Decide on 2 other places to put clues. You want to have three clues to solve the math puzzle treasure map.

3. Figure out how many steps and what directions to turn to get to each place. Make up a math equation to tell how many steps to take.

Look at this example: Suppose you decided to hide the treasure under the teacher's desk in your classroom. Let's say you decided to hide clues on the shelf and under the chalkboard ledge.

The Map:

Clue 1: Start at the desk with an "x" on it. Take (10 - 4) steps toward the shelves to find Clue 2.

Clue 2: Turn to your right. Go (100 - 98) steps to the right of the teacher's desk. Turn left. Walk (3 + 2) steps forward to find Clue 3.

Clue 3: Turn left. Walk ahead (3 + 2 + 3) steps. Look up and down for the treasure.

Tip:

Work with a partner to help you write down and count the correct number of steps. Then, create the math puzzles.

How did I do?   Yes   No

A friend did follow my clues and found the treasure.   ___   ___

MATHEMATICS
Independent Activity

Timing Around

You will get better at thinking of ideas, using a stop watch, arranging things in order.
You will need: a stopwatch, pencil, tally sheet, maybe some friends to help

Activity:

Think of things that can be timed. For example, how long does it take to walk to the principal's office, or slide down a slide? Think of as many as you can. Choose 10 from your list and time how long it actually takes to do those 10 things.

When you have finished, make a chart arranging the activities in order from the slowest (took the most time) to the fastest (took the shortest time). Make your chart exciting by giving it a name and drawing pictures around the edges. Hang it in the hallway for others to see.

Tips:

- Ask a friend to help you with the timing. Your friend can do the activities while you run the stopwatch.
- If you have never used a stopwatch before, have an adult show you how and practice a bit before you begin your experiment.
- If you don't know how to write time in minutes and seconds, ask an adult to show you.

How did I do?

	Yes	No
I thought of 10 interesting things to time.	___	___
I arranged them in order from slowest to fastest.	___	___
My classmates find my chart interesting.	___	___
I could teach someone how to use a stopwatch and write time in minutes and seconds.	___	___

MATHEMATICS
Independent Activity

Fashion Design

You will get better at seeing shapes and using them in new ways.
You will need: construction paper shapes, markers, paper and paste

Activity:

You have just been hired to design a new line of clothes to wear in space. The only catch is that you must create these clothes using circles, squares, rectangles and triangles.

Design at least three outfits. One may be made of only circles. One will be made of only squares and triangles. The last may be made of any shape you choose. Display your designs on construction paper.

Tip:

Try moving the construction paper shapes around before you paste them in place. You may get a good idea once you see it.

How did I do?   Yes   No

My designs use the right shapes.   ____   ____

My designs look interesting—not ordinary. ____   ____

I used the shapes in unusual ways.   ____   ____

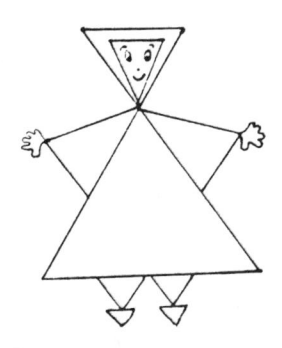

41

MATHEMATICS
Independent Activity

Stump the Riddler

You will get better at describing numbers.
You will need: paper, pens, flexible thinking

Activity:

Have you seen Batman on TV? If so, you probably remember one of his enemies who always spoke in riddles. Do you think you could help Batman by giving him some riddles of his own? Batman has challenged the Riddler to a duel of numbers. Batman needs some numbers to stump his foe. Can you invent some?

> The Riddler just threw this one out…
> The number I'm thinking of is smaller than 5
> and equals 10 when combined with 6 and 3.

Do you know the answer? Now, you think of your own riddles for Batman to use. See if you can stump the Riddler.

Tips:

- The answer to the Riddler's riddle is 1.
- Try using a calculator to help you invent some challenging riddles.

How did I do?

	Yes	No
I created several riddles.	___	___
Some of my riddles stumped my friends.	___	___

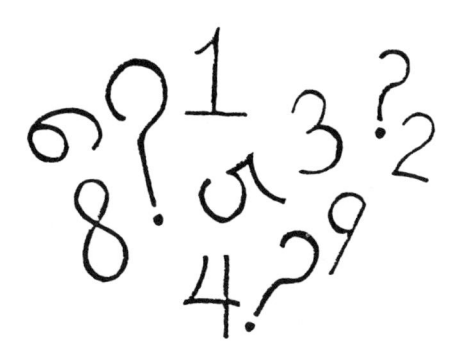

MATHEMATICS
Independent Activity

Squares are Superior

You will get better at supporting your opinions.
You will need: paper and pencil, a friend (You may rather have 2 teams of 3 players each.)

Activity:
Challenge a partner to a brainstorming duel. Each of you picks a different shape. Then, on your own, list all the reasons why your shape is the best. The winner is the one with the most reasons.

Tips:
- Remember to have many ideas; you need to think about silly ones, too.
- When you are out of ideas, take a break and go back to list-making later.
- If you don't know how to write your reason in words, draw a picture of your reason so you won't forget it.

How did I do?

		Yes	No
I thought of at least 10 ideas.	Great!	___	___
I thought of at least 20 ideas.	Fantastic!	___	___
I thought of 50 or more ideas.		___	___
Supercalifragilistic-expialidocious		___	___

or

WOW!

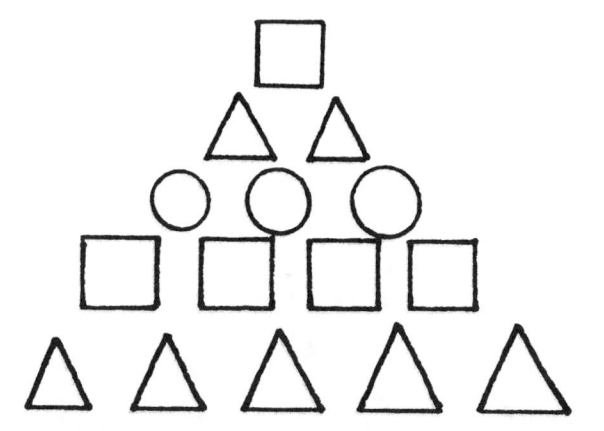

Creative Project For the Math Buff

Title: Games to Learn By

Some children have a hard time learning their math facts. Even though they practice with flash cards and do lots of worksheets, they still may have trouble. Soon, they may begin to hate math because it's just not lots of fun. Because you are so good at math, perhaps you can make up a game to help children with addition.

Idea: Design your own board game to help students learn to add.

Get Ready...

- Are you good at math?
- Do you like to play board games?
- Have you played different kinds?
- Do you like to make things?

Get Set...

- Look at different games for ideas.
- Can you model your game after one you've seen by changing the spinner or cards?
- Get materials together: poster board, markers, index cards, glue. Will you make a spinner, use dice, or color cards? What will you use for game pieces or markers? Keep these materials together in a box with your name on it.
- Ask your teacher where you can work and when you can work.

Go!

The Plan:

Do First:
1. What kind of game will it be?
2. Where can you put in addition?
3. Will you have a theme like Space Hunt or Circus Parade? The theme will help you name your game.
4. Draw a little sketch of what you want the board to look like.

Then:
1. Use your sketch to make your game board. You may want to use pencil first and go over it with markers.
2. Make game pieces.
3. Write the rules of the game.

Finally:
1. Ask your teacher if she can laminate the board and other paper pieces to protect the game.
2. Find a box to keep it in. You may need to fold the game board.
3. Try the game with friends to see if it works. If so, carefully write rules on inside cover of box. If the game isn't quite right, change the rules and then print them on the box. Put the name of the game on outside cover of box.

Quality Control:

- ☐ Does your game require the players to add?
- ☐ Are the directions clear?
- ☐ Are all the pieces in the box?
- ☐ Is your game colorful and pleasing to look at?

If you answered "yes" to the Quality Control Sheet, you are ready to share your game. Let first grade teachers see your game, and have them suggest students who should play it.

Creative Project For the Math Buff

Title: Shopping Spree

Isn't it fun to spend money! The only problem is that there is never enough money for all the things we may wish for! If you accept today's challenge, you will get to go on a make-believe shopping spree. Because you are so good at spending money carefully, you will be in charge of 4 shopping lists: one for you; one for a 4-year-old child; one for your grandmother; and one for a pet cat.

Idea: Create 4 shopping lists. You have $20.00 to spend for each person or pet.

Get Ready...

- Do you like to spend money?

- Are you good at adding and subtracting?

- Can you use a calculator?

- Are you good at spotting bargains?

Get Set...

- Brainstorm items for each list. You may want to interview a 4-year-old, about toys, favorite foods, or books to help you choose. You may need to interview a grandmother, too. Interviewing a cat owner for cat preferences will also give you ideas.

- Get paper for your lists and a sharp pencil to carefully write down prices. A calculator will also help in figuring out your budget.

- Ask your parents for Sunday's paper — the one with advertisements from stores in your area.

Go!

The Plan:

Do First:

1. Look through pages of ads to find things for the 4 lists. Cut them out with the price included.
2. Make a separate pile for each list.

Then:

1. Take one pile at a time. Eliminate items that cost more than $20.00.
2. From the items left, decide which you will buy.
3. Use the calculator to add up prices as you go along.

Finally:

1. When you are happy with your selections, write up your lists of items.
2. Put the price next to each one.
3. Make sure each list has the correct items.

Now with all your skills, you can help grown-ups with their shopping lists. You can become a financial planner.

Quality Control:

☐ Do the items on each list match the items on the wish list?
☐ Was your total amount for all items $20.00 or less?

Creative Project For the Math Buff

Title: Travel Agency, Inc.

Do you like to go on trips with your family? It's fun visiting new places and seeing new things. Another thing that is fun is planning the trip. Because there are so many places to visit and so many ways to get there, trip planning can be an exciting challenge! In this activity, you will plan several different trips for a neat vacation. You will be acting just like a real travel agent.

Idea: You will plan a vacation to a place you would like to visit in the U.S.A. You will develop 2 different plans. Each plan will have its own way to get there and back, places to visit or things to do.

Get Ready...

- Can you read maps?

- Have you heard of or seen places in the U.S.A. that you'd like to visit?

- Ask your parents to take you to a travel agency, where an agent can tell you how she plans a trip.

- Take home some travel brochures to get some ideas.

Get Set...

- Go to the school library and ask the librarian to show you some books about exciting places in the U.S.A.

- Look the books over. Ask friends and relatives about exciting places they have visited.

- Decide where you want to go.

- Get an up-to-date road atlas from the library.

Go!

The Plan:

Do First:

1. Find the place on a map.
2. List all the ways to get there.
   1. Airplane? Is there an airport in that city? There is usually a symbol on a map that shows you where airports are located.
   2. Can you get there by car? Are there good highways to take?
   3. Can you take a boat? How about a train (Call Amtrak or ask your travel agent.)

Then:

Decide which kind of transportation you will use for Plan A. Do research to fill out your "Trip Tick" (see example) for Plan A and Plan B. Use atlases, travel books, and brochures to plan an interesting trip. There should be several stops along the way and back again.

Finally: Fill in Trip Ticks

(on back of TRIP TICK #1)

TRIP TICK # 1
- Destination: Orlando, Florida
- Starting Spot: New York City
- Transportation: Car
- Route: 1. I-95 to Washington, DC
  2. _____
- Stops: 1. Washington, DC {Capitol Bldg, Wash. Mon.}
  2. Savanah, Georgia {Pirate House}

TRIP TICK #2
- Destination: Orlando, Florida
- Starting Spot: New York City
- Transportation: Plane
- Route: 1. Kennedy Airport to Philadelphia Airport
  2. Philadelphia to Atlanta
  3. Atlanta to Orlando
- Stops: 1. Philadelphia, PA
  2. Atlanta, Georgia

RETURN TRIP #1
- Destination: New York City
- Starting Spot: Orlando, Florida
- Transportation: Car
- Route: 1. Florida Turnpike (N) to I-75
  2. I-75 N to Atlanta
  3. _____
- Stops: 1. Atlanta, Georgia {Atlanta Braves baseball game}
  2. _____

Quality Control:

☐ Is your trip exciting?
☐ Did you list things to do or places to see?
☐ Would you like to go on the trip?

Did you enjoy planning these trips? If so, tell your family and friends to let you plan their vacation. After all, you are an expert!

Creative Project For the Math Buff

Title: Survey Specialist

When you are watching television, have you ever heard commercials that say, "Nine out of ten people prefer Colgate Toothpaste" or " 3 out of 4 people prefer Coke to Pepsi?" How do the people who write these commercials know this? Where do they get their information? What they do is take a survey! This is called Market Research. In this activity, you will have the opportunity to conduct your own research to find out about people's likes and dislikes. You can use this information to make up your own commercial or research article.

Idea: Take a survey to find out what kind of cereal kids in your grade like.

Get Ready...

- Do you like to interview people?

- Are you curious about things?

- Do you like math?

- Do you like to tell people what you find out?

Get Set...

- Collect the materials you'll need: index cards, lined paper or graph paper with big blocks, a ruler, crayons or markers.

- Ask your teacher when you can have a few minutes to ask the class to write down their favorite cereal on index cards that you will pass out.

Go!

The Plan:

Do First:

1. Ask everyone in your class to write down the name of their favorite cereal on an index card.

Then:

1. Sort cards into piles according to choice. There maybe a Rice Krispies pile; a Honeycombs pile. Some piles will have lots of cards; others will have only one. Count the number of cards in each pile and put the totals on Tally Sheet.
2. Make a bar graph of your findings like the one below. Used lined paper and color in spaces to match tallies.
3. Looking at your graph you can see which cereal is the favorite. Let's pretend that out of the 25 children in your class, 15 picked Frosted Flakes. Because 15 was the highest number, you can say: Frosted Flakes is the favorite cereal in my class. 15 out of 25 liked that cereal best.

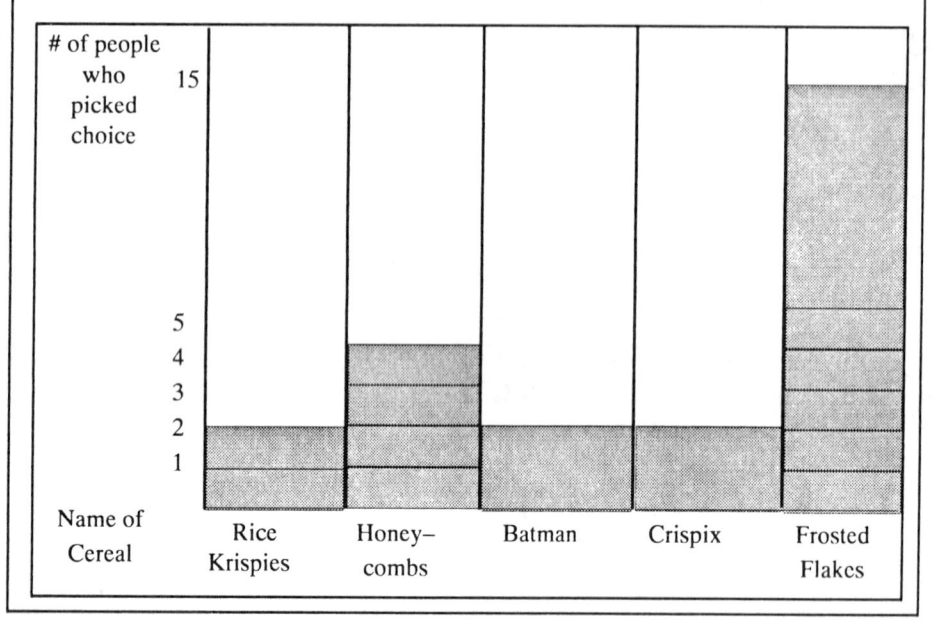

TALLEY SHEET

CATEGORY	How Many?	Final Count
Frosted Flakes	//// //// ////	15
Crispix	//	2

Finally:

Now it's time to use the results. Here are some choices.

1. Make up a magazine ad for the winning cereal, using your results.
2. Write a letter to the company that makes the cereal about the results.
3. Get a box of the cereal and look at the ingredients. Did the children make a healthy choice? Make a poster to congratulate them if that's true. On the other hand, maybe their favorite is not a healthy choice. If so make a poster to convince them to switch cereals.

Quality Control:

☐ Is your survey accurate (Did you count and record correctly?)
☐ Is your graph correct?
☐ Did you use the information to communicate your results?

Did you have fun doing this? If so, you may wish to take more surveys about other things. Remember to communicate your results!

Tally Sheet

Name: _____

Date: _____

Question: _____

CATEGORY	HOW MANY?	FINAL COUNT

What I found out: _____

_____

_____

_____

SCIENCE
Class Activity

Chickens Aren't the Only Ones

Science Objective: classification
Creativity Objective: flexibility, originality
Materials Needed: The books, *Chickens aren't the only ones* and *Scroobious Pip**, chalkboard, chalk

Activity:

Read *Chickens aren't the only ones* and discuss the concepts of classification and grouping. Point out that many things can be grouped. Act as scribe as the children brainstorm to create a list of all the living things they can think of. Review the list and ask them to try grouping things on the list. After they build groups, have them identify the common attribute(s) of the members of the group and name the group.

The next day, read *Scroobious Pip*. Have the children think of ideas of what to do with a creature which can't be grouped. Return to their list. Did they have any which couldn't be grouped? Can they group it now?

Extension:

Have the children make up a new class of creatures with some unique attribute in common. Create a display of this new classification and the creatures of this new class.

* Heller, R. (1981). *Chickens aren't the only ones.* NY: Grosset & Dunlap.
Lear, E. (1968). *Scroobious Pip.* NY: Harper & Row.

SCIENCE
Class Activity

Talking Without Words

Science Objective: observation skills, animal behavior patterns
Creativity Objective: flexibility
Materials Needed: notebooks and pencils

Activity:

Go for a nature walk on the school grounds, wooded area or nearby park. Have pairs of students watch for signs of how animals and plants help each other. Have them record their observations in their notebooks.

Extension:

- Drama: They could act out some of their observations.
- They could draw pictures of what they saw.

SCIENCE
Class Activity

Staying Safe

Science Objective: survival, fact and fiction
Creativity Objective: elaboration
Materials Needed: drawing paper, markers, chart paper

Activity:

Make a list with the class of how animals protect themselves. Include ideas of how humans protect themselves, as well.

For example: skunks--aroma, cheetahs--speed, salamanders--change color, children--hide.

Following the discussion, cut out the names of the animals, and put them in one bag. Cut out the protective behaviors, and put them in another bag. Allow the children to take turns randomly choosing one slip from each bag. Then, ask them to write a story about the animal and its protective behavior. Some of the combinations will be possible. Others will be silly. This can lead to a discussion of fiction and non-fiction writing.

Extension:

Invent a protective device for people based on animal behaviors, e.g., clothes that change color.

SCIENCE
Class Activity

Grabbing Health

Science Objective: nutrition and safety rules
Creativity Objective: originality, elaboration
Materials Needed: poster board, thick markers or poster paint

Activity:

Tell the class thay are part of a campaign to convince people to live a healthful life. Brainstorm all the things we should do to keep healthy. Have small groups choose one idea and develop a poster to promote the idea. Place the posters in a local supermarket, bank or other public spot.

Extension:

Have the children write and conduct a survey to find out how people are following health and safety rules. They can graph their results.

SCIENCE
Class Activity

To Float or Not to Float

Science Objective: properties of air, principles of invention
Creativity Objective: problem solving, flexibility
Materials Needed: raisins, clear plastic cups, warm bottles of 7-up, water, lab sheet, drawing paper

Activity:

Ask the children what would happen if they dropped raisins into seven-up. Some will say they will float. Some will predict they will sink. Give pairs of students 2 cups. Fill one cup 2/3 full with 7-up. (Make sure the seven-up is not flat.) Have the children observe and record what they see on a science observation sheet (see p. 61).

Give the children time to brainstorm why the raisins dance up and down. Lead them to notice the bubbles. Have them decide how to prove that the bubbles made of air cling to and lift the raisins. They will need to use the other cup to try raisins in other liquids without carbonation to test their ideas.

After they conclude that air can lift things, have them draw an invention that uses air to help them float in water (see p. 62). Tell them to name their invention and decorate it to make it attractive to others.

Extension:

Set up an invention center in the classroom.

Science Observation Sheet

Problem: If we put raisins in a glass of 7-Up, what do you think will happen?

       sink   float

Observation: Watch the raisins closely for a few minutes. What do you see?

1. _____
2. _____
3. _____

Hypothesis: Why do you think the raisins did that?

_____
_____
_____

Testing the hypothesis: How can you find out if your hunch was right? What will you do?

What will you need?

Observation: What happened?

_____

Rule: What rule or property about air did you discover?

_____

Application

Given that air can lift solids, can you invent something to help you float in water? Remember to use the new rule about air in your invention.

What can you add to your invention to make it sell?

SCIENCE
Class Activity

Science Snooper

Science Objective: observation, questioning skills
Creativity Objective: fluency, flexibility, originality, problem solving
Materials Needed: a pond, notebook, pencil

Activity:

Have the children sit quietly at a pond. Have them identify the sounds, colors, sensations, and smells they sense in 5 minutes. Next, have them list 10 questions about their observations. Encourage them to ask questions to which they do not have the answers.

Upon returning to the classroom, discuss how many different questions they came up with (fluency), what categories did they use (flexibility), who asked a question no one else thought of (originality). Help them talk about their questions and answer them. Give them a "Good Thinker" certificate.

Extension:

Have the children research the answers to some of their more interesting questions.

SCIENCE
Independent Activity

Name That Tune!

You will get better at hearing sounds and writing your own songs.
You will need: 8 water glasses that are all the same size, water, spoon, ruler, marker

Activity:

Take the glasses and use your ruler to mark them as follows:

#1 — place a mark at 1/2 inch.

#2 — place a mark at 1 inch.

#3 — place a mark at 1 1/2 inches.

#4 — place a mark at 2 inches.

#5 — place a mark at 2 1/2 inches.

#6 — place a mark at 3 inches.

#7 — place a mark at 3 1/2 inches.

#8 — place a mark at 4 inches.

Fill each glass with water up to the mark you made. Hit each glass gently with the spoon. What do you hear? Do the glasses with high notes have more or less water in them?

Now, create your own melody by tapping your glasses. Write down the numbers of the glasses to record your tune. Like this:

1 1 3 3 2 4 1

1 1 4 4 3 3 2

1 4 3 8 1 4 3 8

2 2 2

Let your friends play your tune. Put words to your tune.

Tip:

Use patterns of numbers. What do they sound like?

How did I do?   Yes   No

I could write a tune.   ____   ____

Others could play my tune by reading my musical score.   ____   ____

SCIENCE
Independent Activity

Spaced Out Planets

You will get better at writing science fiction and thinking of original ideas.
You will need: a shoe box, junk to build with, glue and paper

Activity:

Invent a new planet and brainstorm all its characteristics. Include: temperature, amount of gravity, hours of night, hours of day, creatures who live there.

Make a shadow box scene in your showbox showing life on your planet.

Tip:

It's fun to take a risk and think of things no one else thinks of.

How did I do?

	Yes	No
My scene matches the characteristics I invented for my planet.	___	___
I like my shadowbox scene.	___	___

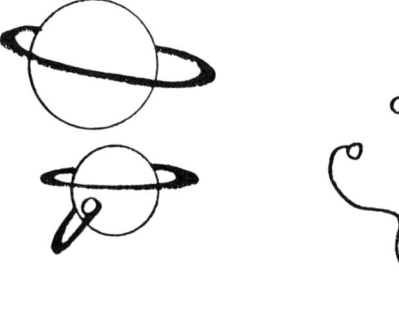

SCIENCE
Independent Activity

Menu Madness

You will get better at creatively planning healthy meals.
You will need: construction paper, markers, magazines, scissors, a list of the 4 food groups

Activity:

Invent a sandwich for every day of the week. The sandwich must appeal to children and represent all four food groups. Give your sandwich a name and create an attractive menu to advertise your week of lunches.

Tips:

List food from each food group. Survey your class to see what foods they like from each group. Use their favorites in inventing your sandwiches.

How did I do?

	Yes	No
My friends like my menu.	___	___
Some people tried some of my ideas.	___	___

(See if your friends want to plan a wacky sandwich day to try unusual sandwiches.)

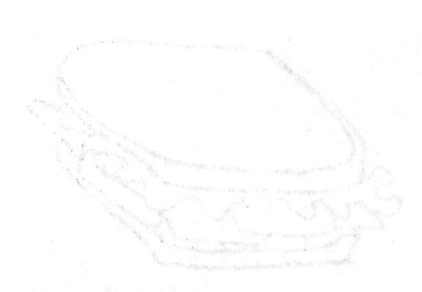

SCIENCE
Independent Activity

Picture This

You will get better at figuring out the parts of a story. You will learn how a seed changes into a flower.

You will need: several lima beans, a wet sponge, a jar, a camera with film

Activity:

Place your sponge in the jar and place the beans between the sponge and the sides of the jar. Keep the jar in a dark place. Check your jar every day to be sure the sponge is still damp. If it dries out put a little water in to make it damp again.. Take a picture of the jar every day until the roots are formed. When a stem with leaves is formed , place the jar in the light. Transplant the baby plants (Be very gentle!) into pots with dirt. Have your pictures developed.

Use your pictures to show how a seed becomes a plant.

Tip:

You could make a chart, game or picture book from your pictures.

How did I do?   Yes   No

My plant grew.   ____   ____

My pictures show how a seed changes into a plant.   ____   ____

I can explain how a seed changes into a plant.   ____   ____

SCIENCE
Independent Activity

The Play's the Thing

You will get better at choosing good food to eat. You will also be better at writing a short skit.
You will need: a book about healthy foods, paper, pencil

Activity:

Write a short skit about eating good foods. You can use puppets or real people to perform your play. Remember to write down who the characters are, where the skit takes place, the time of day, and what the actors should say during the skit.

Tips:

You might want one of the characters to need some help in picking healthy foods.

You could have food be the characters — a talking carrot?!

How did I do?   Yes   No

My skit teaches people about healthy foods.   ____   ____

I used interesting characters.   ____   ____

I wrote interesting speeches for my characters.   ____   ____

SCIENCE
Independent Activity

I Spy

You will get better at observing things.
You will need: a 1 foot by 1 foot plot of lawn, 4 sticks, string, ruler, notebook, pencil, magnifying glass

Activity:

Measure a plot of lawn that is 1 foot by 1 foot. Put the sticks in at each corner, and tie your string so it makes a little fence around your plot. Look carefully in your plot. Make a map of your plot and a list of the things you see there. Be sure to use your magnifying glass to notice the tiny things. Check your plot every day for four days. Write down any changes.

Make a drawing of the plot and what you saw in your plot.

Tip:

Be patient. Look for bugs, leaves, rocks, different grasses.

How did I do?   Yes   No

I noticed many things. I was a fluent thinker.   ____   ____

I noticed different things. I was a flexible thinker.   ____   ____

I noticed strange things. I was a good observer.   ____   ____

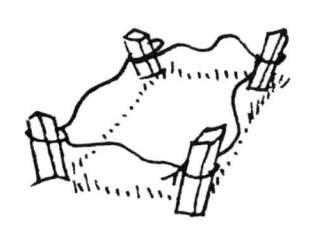

Creative Project For the Science Buff

Title: Seasonal Stroll

Which season do you like best? All of us have our favorites. Sometimes it's really hard to choose a favorite because each season offers its own brand of beauty. This project will help you discover the secrets of each season as you take a stroll along a nature walk.

Idea: A slide show on changing seasons with a musical background.

Get Ready...

- Do you have a favorite spot where you go to see nature?

- Do you know how to use a camera?

- Do you listen to music that makes you feel peaceful and calm?

Get Set...

- You will need an adult assistant who has a good camera. This adult can help YOU take pictures and accompany you on your walk.

- You will need color slide film. (4 rolls)

- You will need to listen to tapes or records of peaceful music.

- You will need the whole year to do this. Get started by October.

Go!

The Plan:

Do First:

1. Find a pretty place
   1. Pond
   2. Park
   3. Path into woods
   4. Stone wall
   5. Brook or stream

2. Practice taking pictures. Ask your adult assistant to teach you how. Be flexible.

Then:

Take a walk in fall. Snap pictures of this favorite place. Use a whole roll. Have pictures developed.

Go back in winter, when snow covers the ground. Shoot another roll of the same scene. Have the pictures developed.

Return again in early spring when buds are on the trees.

And once more in early June.

Finally:

Select the best slides of each season. Choose the peaceful music you like best. Make a tape of music. Have your adult assistant show you how to make a title and credits slide.

Quality Control:

☐ Are the pictures clear?
☐ Have I enough pictures for each season?
☐ Is the music pleasing?

If you passed quality control, you are ready to present your photo study.

Bravo!

Creative Project For the Science Buff

Title: Ecology Watch

Do you have any idea how much water we waste each day? Living things cannot live without water. We must take care to conserve our water supply. You can help. In this activity you will be asked to design a checklist for families who want to save water.

Idea: Design a water conservation checklist.

Get Ready...

- Do you know a lot about saving water? If not, get some books from the library.

- Can you use a computer? Do you know how to do word-processing?

Get Set...

- You will need to use a computer. You will need a notebook, pencil, and a camera if possible.

Go!

The Plan:

Do First:
1. Visit the homes of 10 of your friends and relatives.
2. Note in what ways they waste water.
3. Jot down signs of water waste. Photograph some, if you can.

Then:
1. Make a list of all the ways you've noticed that people waste water.
2. Write for some information from a conservation agency for some ideas. Get the address from rhe Blue Pages of the Phonebook. Or ask the librarian in your town library.
3. Write a tip to go with each way you discovered people waste water.

Finally:
1. Pick 10 tips that you think will work.
2. Type them on the computer. Have the computer teacher help you design a good looking checklist.
3. Try it out in your house to see if your ideas work.

Quality Control:
☐ Did you find ways that people waste water?
☐ Did you have tips to help them stop?
☐ Does your checklist look nice?
☐ Did your trial run work?

If you are pleased with the result, have copies made of your checklist.

Pass them out at P.T.A meetings, supermarkets, and other places.

Creative Project For the Science Buff

Title: Sliding In

Have you ever noticed how many "riders" the slide on the playground has in a day? Not everything that takes a ride down the slide is human. Some shoes, dolls, balls, and matchbox cars take a trip down the slide, set loose by their owners. Have you seen things that just don't go down a regular slide? Some things just stick. Well, that's how your problem starts...

Idea: Design a 3-foot slide for a chalkboard eraser that will allow the eraser a fast trip to the bottom.

Get Ready...

- Do you understand friction?
- Are you a good experimenter?
- Can you think of many solutions to a problem?

Get Set...

- Try a number of different things on a slide.
- Figure out why some things go fast and others go slowly.
- Think of at least 6 things you could do to let an eraser have a fast trip down a slide.
- Gather the materials you need to test your 6 ideas.

Go!

The Plan:

Do First:
Test your Ideas
1. Make the 3-foot slide and the eraser changes.
2. Test each idea several times.
3. Decide which ideas are the best.
4. Pick your best 2 ideas.

Then:
1. Make any changes in your 2 ideas to make them any better.
2. Time 3 trials for each idea.
3. See which idea produces the fastest results.

Finally:
1. Challenge another slide engineer to a race.
2. Have 3 trials, and time the races.
3. Determine the winner.

Quality Control:

☐ Did you find out about friction to help you understand how "slides" work?
☐ Did you think of changing the slide surface? the eraser?
☐ Did you test <u>different</u> ideas or similar ideas?
☐ Were you a good sport at the challenge?

Creative Project For the Science Buff

Title: Cloudy Day

Have you ever seen flying lions or floating mountains? If you lie on your back and look up at the sky on a sunny day with clouds in the sky, you might. Clouds can look like many things. They can also give us messages if we know how to read them.

Idea: Observe what clouds mean by keeping a weather chart, and figure out how to "read" the clouds.

Get Ready…

- Make a recording book for your observations (see below).

- You will need to keep your observation book with pages for 1 month of observations.

- Practice drawing clouds so they look like the clouds in the sky on different days.

Observation Sheet
Date: _____
Time: _____

Next day it was _____

Get Set…

- Decide when you want to start your month of cloud watching.

- Decide what time of day you'll do your observations.

Go!

The Plan:

Do First:

1. Begin by doing your observation and drawing a picture of the sky just as it looks.
2. The next day, before you draw the picture of the sky, tell what the weather is. Write it at the bottom of the page of yesterday's observation. Then, draw your picture of today's sky.
3. Repeat this every day for the month.

Then:

1. Study your drawings.
2. See if certain shapes or kinds of clouds always (or usually) appeared before certain kinds of weather.
3. Complete this chart.

When clouds look like:	Tomorrow will be:

Finally:

1. Predict the weather for 10 days by using your chart.
2. Keep track of how often you are correct.

Quality Control:

☐ I found some patterns in my cloud—weather book.
☐ My drawings show how clouds are different.
☐ I think I know what clouds tell us about the weather.

SOCIAL STUDIES
Class Activity

Our History

Social Studies Objective: development of a sense of how history is written, reporting and summarizing.

Creativity Objective: fluency, elaboration

Materials Needed: album, camera, markers

Activity:

Divide the class into groups of four or five. Whenever a special day or event is planned, assign one of the history groups to chronicle the event. Before the event, meet with the group to discuss their ideas. They might photograph, draw, interview, or collect things to remember the event. They will have one page in the album to design. At the end of the year, bind the book and place it in the library.

Extension:

- Do an annual school history book of school events.
- Ask a parent to serve as class historian and work with the history groups to create the pages in the album.

SOCIAL STUDIES
Class Activity

My History

Social Studies Objective: recognition of history through biography; writing a chronology

Creativity Objective: elaboration

Materials Needed: 2 short biographies (stories, articles, character sketches)

Activity:

Discuss biographies so the children know that they are recounting of a particular person's life. Talk to the children about their lives and what they would like to have in their life stories. Have each child make a list of the things he or she would want in a biography. Have them write their auto biographies. Encourage them to use pictures, interviews, artifacts to make their autobiography interesting.

Extension:

- Write a pet's biography.
- Write a parent's or grandparent's biography.

SOCIAL STUDIES
Class Activity

Special Studies

Social Studies Objective: recognition of family and cultural differences and patterns

Creativity Objective: flexibility

Materials Needed: magazines, newspapers, advertising flyers

Activity:

Discuss how food likes and dislikes change over time (babies to childhood to adulthood, frontier days to now) and how families have different ideas to "special treats." Have the children interview their family members about their favorite foods. They can then find or draw pictures of their family treats and make a mobile. Discuss the common and the unique foods shown on the mobiles.

Extension:

- Interview a variety of people (of all ages) about their favorite food treat when they were the same ages as the children. Make a bar graph or a mobile of the findings.
- Have a special treat day to celebrate family foods.

SOCIAL STUDIES
Class Activity

Different or Same

Social Studies Objective: recognition of change and continuity
Creativity Objective: fluency, flexibility
Materials Needed: collection of magazines, newspapers, catalogues, school books for the present and from the years the children were born

Activity:

Allow the children to investigate the print material noting how things have changed and what things have remained the same. They might note differences in appliances, furniture, clothes, hair styles and continuity in kinds of advertising. They might notice different kinds of stories but many of the same words in the school books.

Have them do a "Then and Now" chart to compare and contrast their findings.

Extension:

- Have the children add a "Futures" piece to their chart, predicting what will change and what will remain the same in the next _____ years.

SOCIAL STUDIES
Class Activity

Family Mapping

Social Studies Objective: recognition of genealogy and family roots
Creativity Objective: elaboration
Materials Needed: maps, globes

Activity:

After discussing and examining different scales of maps (world, country, regional, state, town) have the children find out the birth places of all their family members (parents, siblings, grandparents, aunts, uncles, cousins) and mark them in an appropriate map. Have them make a "family circle" which encompasses all their family members. Discuss the different circles. Some will be within a state. Some will be within a region. Others will be international.

Have them write a story about two people in their family and the places those two were born.

Extension:
- Make a birthplace collage about the birth places of family members.

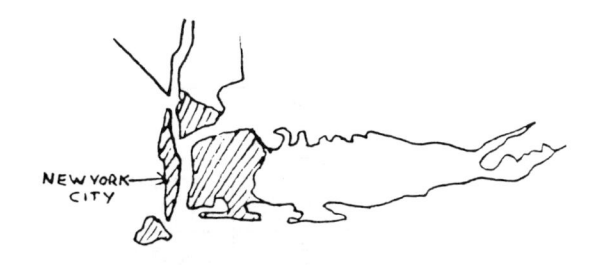

SOCIAL STUDIES
Class Activity

In Our Town

Social Studies Objective: career awareness
Creativity Objective: flexibility
Materials Needed: telephone books

Activity:

Begin by brainstorming all the careers the children know. Circle all those listed the children believe are available in their town.

Using the telephone book, have groups of children add to the list and tally the number of businesses in career areas, e.g., 15 doctors, 8 plumbers, 12 electricians, 6 veterinarians.

Graph the 15 most listed careers.

Extension:

- Design a special graph which shows the professions in a unique way, e.g., show the veterinarians in a pictograph using a cat face for every vet.

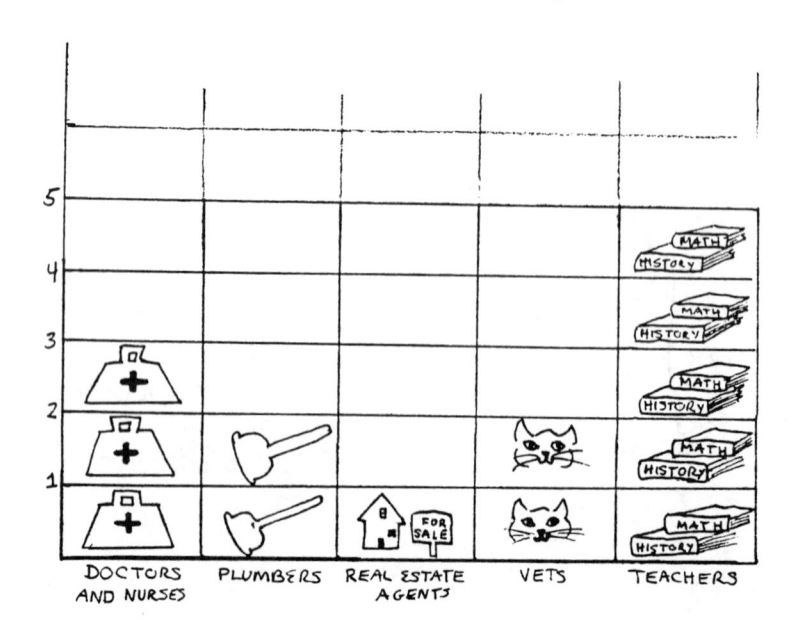

SOCIAL STUDIES
Independent Activity

Match Box Parade

You will get better at: planning a report

You will need: a match box car, decorations of your choice

Activity:

After learning information in a social studies unit (for example — explorers, community helpers, holidays), pretend you are in charge of a parade for wee people. Your job is to design a float that shows them something you have learned. The trick is — you will show them by designing a float your match box car can pull. Decide what important thing you learned and design a float for your wee people parade.

Tips:

- You could use legos for your float platform.
- Try to show one main idea (not everything you learned).
- Design your float on paper, then work on building it.

How did I do?   Yes   No

My float looks good.   ___   ___

My friends understood what my idea was.   ___   ___

My car pulled my float.   ___   ___

SOCIAL STUDIES
Independent Activity

Favorite Days

You will get better at: planning projects, understanding celebrations.

You will need: library information, project materials of your choice

Activity:

We all celebrate holidays. Some are religious holidays. Some are family holidays. Some are for our country. Make a list of things we celebrate and don't forget special family celebrations like your birthday. Choose a favorite holiday to investigate.

Using library information and talking to other people, find out all you can about your special day. Answer questions such as:

1. Why do we celebrate this day?
2. Who celebrates this day?
3. How do we celebrate it?
4. When did this celebration begin?

Write a short story about your special day. Be sure to include your important information. Then, design a project which shows people celebrating your holiday. You might choose a diorama, a mobile, a mural or a model. Can you think of another kind of project?

Tips:

- Check with your school or town librarian for help in finding information.
- Talk to several people to find out the different ways they celebrate.

How did I do?

	Yes	No
I found out some interesting information.	___	___
My project looks as good as I thought it would.	___	___
Readers understand my holiday story.	___	___

SOCIAL STUDIES
Independent Activity

Toy Stories

You will get better at: finding information, seeing changes, making predictions.
You will need: library books, books on toys, mural paper, paints or markers

Activity:

Children have always liked toys, but the toys have not always stayed the same. Some toys have been favorites for a long time — like Raggedy Ann and Andy, blocks and teddy bears. Others are new — like masters of the Universe and Slime. Some toys have different looks — like dolls such as cornhusk dolls, rag dolls and Barbie.

List five of your favorite toys that you would like to study. Investigate their history so you know:

- When were your toys invented?
- How have they changed since they were invented?
- Who likes playing with them?

Make a time line for your toys showing how they have changed.* Do a survey to find out who plays with them, and show your results on a bar graph.

Tips:

- Do a survey of your classmates to find out who plays with the toys on your list. Use graph paper to make your bar graph. (Ask your teacher or your parents to help you if you have never done a bar graph before.)
- If you have trouble finding the history of one of your toys, write a letter to the company who makes it. Ask them your questions.
- Make a chart to keep your information organized.

How did I do?

	Yes	No
I picked some old and some new toys.	___	___
I found some interesting changes.	___	___
My bar graph looks interesting.	___	___
My time lines show the changes in my toys nicely.	___	___

*Sample Time line Organizer p. 96.

Time Line Organizer

Name: _____

Date: _____

1. List of Toys   **When they were used (get dates)**

_____   _____
_____   _____
_____   _____
_____   _____
_____   _____
_____   _____
_____   _____
_____   _____

2. Place the events in order on the time line.

SOCIAL STUDIES
Independent Activity

Guess Where

You will get better at: brainstorming, investigating, observing, looking at parts of things.
You will need: a picture of a famous place, clue cards, magnifying glass

Activity:

With the help of your teacher or your parents, think of a famous place. Find a picture of that place. Examine your picture carefully. Use the magnifying glass to see all you can. Make a copy of your picture in the Xerox machine so your picture won't be ruined in the next step.

Using the copy of your picture, place a piece of tracing paper over it. Mark at least four cutout places which would allow peeks of your place. Try to design peeks which give a clue without giving the whole thing away. For example, if your place was a MacDonalds— showing the golden arches would give it away but showing a person eating a hamburger might be a good clue.

Once you have decided and marked your peek-a-boo clues on the tracing paper, cut them out. Put the tracing paper on a piece of construction paper and trace the cut outs. Cut them out and then tape little doors over the cutouts so no one can see the clues.

Tape the construction paper cover and your picture together and put it on a bulletin board. Check to see if the doors cover the cutouts. Check to see if the cutouts are in the right spots. Now you are ready for the "Guess Where" game.

Remove one of the doors each day unitl someone guesses your place. You might put a guess sheet next to your game so anyone with a guess can put their guess and their name on the sheet. See how many clues they need to guess your famous place. Make a "Good Guesser" ribbon for the person who guessed correctly.

Tips:

- Look in old magazines for pictures of famous places.
- You could do this with a famous person as well.

How did I do?

	Yes	No
I designed good clues.	___	___
I picked a place (person) my classmates knew.	___	___
Someone guessed correctly after seeing some of the clues.	___	___

SOCIAL STUDIES
Independent Activity

Clothes Designer

You will get better at: thinking of original ideas, and recognizing the community helpers in your town.

You will need: paper, crayons or markers, pictures of firefighters, police officers, doctors, mail carriers, veterinarians, other people in work clothes

Activity:

All communities have people whose jobs help others. Collect all the pictures you can showing these helpers at work. Take a careful look at how their work clothes look. Pick one kind of helper and design new work clothes for people with that job. Think about the kind of work and what the worker has to do. What colors would be best? Draw a front and back view of a worker in your new uniform.

Create a display with a community helper collage made of your collection of pictures. Include your new design in the display.

Tips:

- If you're stuck, make a list of jobs your community helper does at work, and think how clothes could help make the work easier or safer. You could talk with someone who really does the work. Ask him or her what changes in work clothes would be helpful.
- Look in newspapers and old magazines for pictures of community helpers at work. Brochures are a good place to look, as well.

How did I do?

	Yes	No
My collage looks good.	___	___
My drawing shows my ideas well.	___	___
My friends understand why I made the changes in the work clothes.	___	___
I like this project.	___	___

Creative Project For the Social Studies Buff

Title: Your Town

Everybody has special memories of his or her hometown. Indeed, every town offers something special to the people who live there. It would be great to have a poster that tells others what is special about your town. The poster can be a photographic essay showing special events, special spots or even people who make your town unique.

Idea: Photographic essay or travel poster about your hometown!

Get Ready...

- Do you have a camera?
- Do you like to take pictures?
- Do you like to talk to people?
- Do you like your town?

Get Set...

- Get an adult to consent to be your assistant for part of your project.
- You will need a camera (35 millimeter is best, but others will do.) and color print film.

Go!

The Plan:

Do First:
1. Ask teachers, parents, friends' parents and/or grandparents to list 3 special places or happenings in your town.
2. Visit people at the Town Hall, and ask them the same. (Here's where your adult assistant comes in handy as driver.)
3. Maybe you could run an ad in the local paper, asking citizens of your town to send you their choices.

Then:
1. Assemble your results. List places mentioned. Keep a tally of how many times each was mentioned.
2. Choose 8-10 of the most popular ideas.
3. With your adult assistant, go out and photograph the spots. Take five pictures of each spot, using different views.

Finally:
1. Get the pictures developed and choose the best ones.
2. Get those pictures enlarged to 5"x7". (Copy stores have a less expensive way of doing this. Ask your adult assistant about it.)
3. Arrange pictures on a large poster board. Label each picture—use stick-on letters—as to what and where each is.
4. Title your essay, using bigger stick-on letters.

Quality Control:

☐ Are the photographs in focus?
☐ Is everything neatly labeled?
☐ Is there a title that includes the name of the town?

If you are happy with your essay, you may wish to:
1. Exhibit your essay in the Town Hall or
2. See if your local paper will publish it or
3. Visit a local printer or copy center about making it into a travel poster.

Creative Project For the Social Studies Buff

Title: The Day You Were Born

Have you ever wondered what happened the day you were born? What kind of music was popular? What was playing on TV? Who was President of the U.S.? How much a candy bar cost? This project will allow you to answer these questions and others, as well.

Idea: Make a picture book comparing the day you were born with the day your mom was born.

Get Ready...

- Do you like to look at photograph albums?

- Do you have a baby book?

- Have you ever kept a scrap book?

Get Set...

- You will need a notebook, a tape recorder and tape, family albums, your baby book, and an adult assistant.

Go!

The Plan:

Do First:

1. Brainstorm questions you have about the day you were born.
2. Ask your mother to think of all the questions she may have about the day she was born.
3. Compare your questions, and decide on 6-10 good questions to work with.

Then:

1. Make a chart to help you decide where to find the answers to your questions.
   The questions go in the left column, and places to find information go across the top. Decide which sources you will need to answer your questions.

2. As you can see, lots of questions can be answered by looking in a newspaper printed on your mom's birthdate. You can get a copy of the newspaper from your library. They have microfilm copies of old newspapers there. You can get a printed copy.

	Newspaper	Interviews	Photo Albums	Baby Book
1. President	X			
2. Cost of Candy Bar	X	X		X
3. Fashions	X		X	
4. Singing Stars	X	X		
5. TV Shows	X			
6. News	X			?
7. What Dad Did		X		?

3. Go to the sources and find the answers to questions. Don't forget your tape recorder for interviews.
4. Keep records in your notebook of what you discover.

Quality Control:

☐ Did you answer your questions?
☐ Did you use at least 3 sources for your research?
☐ Is your book neat and easy to read?

If you answered "yes" to these questions, you are ready to finish your book. Make a cover — include a title, and the name and author. Donate the book to your family library.

Finally:

1. Compile your research for you and your mom in a book.
2. You can do it like the one pictured below or in your own way.

My Birthday: June 1, 1985 — Mom's Birthday: March 19, 1958

In this book each question gets its own full page. One side is for Mom's Birthday, the other is for you. Be creative in decorating each page.

Creative Project For the Social Studies Buff

Title: If my school could talk

Wouldn't it be funny if buildings could talk? They could tell you their own story about their lives. But as you well know, buildings don't talk, but within their walls we can discover many things about their lives. If you like to snoop around, you can find out all about the life of your school. You can be the one to tell its story.

Idea: A talking timeline: The Story of Our School.

Get Ready...

- Do you like to snoop around?

- Do you like to interview people?

- Have you seen the book the *Story of a Castle*?* If not, ask at the library.

Get Set...

- You will need a tape recorder, a camera, a notebook, and sharp pencils. It would be a good idea to "hire" an adult assistant.

Go!

* Goodall, John S. (1986). *The Story of a Castle.* NY: Macmillan.

The Plan:

Do First:

Read the *Story of a Castle*. It can give you some ideas for the Story of Our School.

Brainstorm questions to be answered like:

1. When was your school built?
2. Who was its first principal?
3. Have any children who went there become famous?
4. Who attended?
5. Are there new additions?
6. Special events?
7. Disasters?
8. Happy memories?

	1900 - 10	1911-41	1942-71	1972-92
Principal				
# Students				
Teacher Interviews				
Student Interviews				
Happy Event				
Sad or Disastrous Event				
News Article				

Then:

1. Ask your teacher or adult assistant to find out where you can find answers. The list below will give you some ideas:

    a. Find cornerstone — photograph it. It will tell you the school's date.

    b. Find copies of local newspaper for that year. See if there is an article about the school's opening.

    c. Look at plaques on walls of the school.

    d. Interview: Principal, janitors, teachers who taught in the building the longest.

2. Organize the search. Remember your project is a time line. When you find out the year the school was opened, you can decide what you need to do.

3. Divide your story into clumps like: the 1st 10 years, 2nd 30 years, 3rd 30 years....See example to the left.

Finally:

1. Put all your information onto a mural — butcher paper or a roll of construction paper will do well. Make time line and paste things you've collected like photographs and facts you've learned under the line segment for the right years.

2. Make a tape of you using the information on the time line to tell a story. If you were lucky enough to get interviews, have your adult assistant help put them into your taped story.

Quality Control:

☐ Did you answer most of your questions?
☐ Did you have something for each set of years on your time line?
☐ Does your taped story go with the time line?
☐ Can you understand the tape?

If you have answered "yes" to each of the questions, organize a display of your work for others to see and hear.

Creative Project For the Social Studies Buff

Title: My Birthday Journal

It would be fun for you to keep a journal about you on your birthday — year by year as you grow up. You can start by finding out about your past birthday. Just think how much fun it would be to show this journal to your children some day.

Idea: Birthday Journal

Get Ready...
- Do you have a baby book?
- Do your parents have photos or videos of your birthday parties?
- Are you good at asking questions?

Get Set...
- You will need to make the birthday memory collector kit pictured here. You may want to use a tape recorder, too.
- Last, you will need a scrapbook for your journal.

BIRTHDAY MEMORY COLLECTOR'S KIT

- One big manila envelope

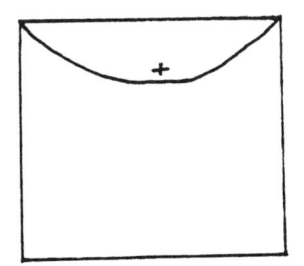

- A smaller one for each birthday you have celebrated.

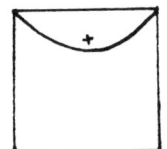

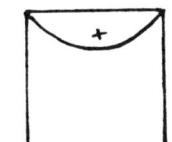

Below is a copy of a Birthday Treasure checklist to paste on front of each small envelope.

Birthday Treasure Checklist

1. Memories from Mom and Dad.
2. A picture of me on my birthday.
3. A list of people who came to my party.
4. What was the theme?
5. Where was the party held?
6. Sample invitation and birthday cards.

Go!

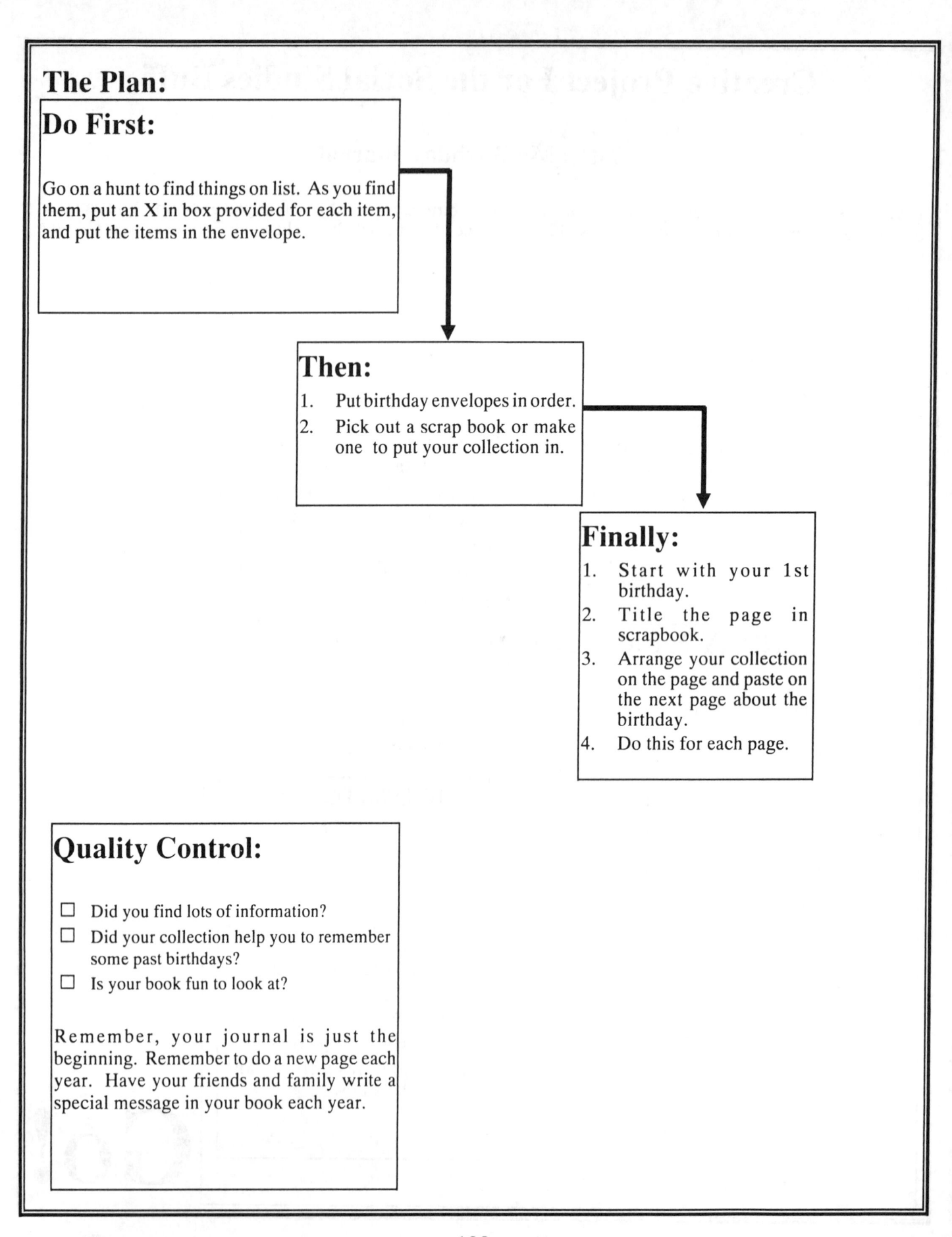

The Plan:

Do First:

Go on a hunt to find things on list. As you find them, put an X in box provided for each item, and put the items in the envelope.

Then:
1. Put birthday envelopes in order.
2. Pick out a scrap book or make one to put your collection in.

Finally:
1. Start with your 1st birthday.
2. Title the page in scrapbook.
3. Arrange your collection on the page and paste on the next page about the birthday.
4. Do this for each page.

Quality Control:

☐ Did you find lots of information?
☐ Did your collection help you to remember some past birthdays?
☐ Is your book fun to look at?

Remember, your journal is just the beginning. Remember to do a new page each year. Have your friends and family write a special message in your book each year.

LANGUAGE ARTS
Class Activity

Center Stage

Language Arts Objective: review of vowel sounds, playwriting
Creativity Objective: originality, elaboration
Materials Needed: paper, pencil, variety of craft materials to make a puppet

Activity:

Divide the class into five groups. Each group chooses a vowel sound and invents an account of why it makes the sound it does. Each group develops a puppet representing its vowel. The stories are combined into a puppet show. Then, have the class brainstorm a title for the production. Invite another class to the play, or consider making a slide and tape production of the play — and circulate it to all kindergartens in the district.

Extensions:

- Puppet theatre — monthly productions.
- Video/slide-tape show of special projects.
- Puppet-making center

LANGUAGE ARTS
Class Activity

The Mouse House

Language Arts Objective: listening comprehension, character analysis
Creativity Objective: originality, elaboration
Materials Needed: story about a mouse, e.g. Country Mouse-City Mouse, The Mouse and the Motorcycle, The Borrowers, variety of craft materials and containers

Activity:

Read the story to the class. Discuss the story and the characters. Have the children work in groups to design a house for one of the characters in the story. The house should relate to the setting of the story with details appropriate to particular character chosen.

Extensions:

- Read other stories and create other houses for special characters.
- Get a pet mouse for the classroom and keep an observation log.
- Write your own class mouse story.

LANGUAGE ARTS
Class Activity

Class Characters

Language Arts Objective: listening, interviewing
Creativity Objective: flexibility, elaboration
Materials Needed: pencil, paper, interview questions, drawing paper, paints or markers

Activity:

Brainstorm a list of interview questions to find out about the experiences, interests, activities of a friend. Have the children pick a partner and have the partners interview each other. Using the information from the interview, have the children draw at least 3 different views of their partner. Allow each person to pick the favorite drawing of him/herself. These drawings can go in a class display. Encourage the children to include details in the drawings which show their partners' interests and activities.

Extensions:

- Read a biography, and have the children draw a series of pictures showing different aspects of the title character.
- Interview teachers in the school, and make a "Teacher" bulletin board showing how teachers spend their time out of school.
- Transfer the drawings to fabric, and make a quilt.

LANGUAGE ARTS
Class Activity

Just Like Me

Language Arts Objective: forming analogies, language development
Creativity Objective: fluency, flexibility
Materials Needed: *Quick as a cricket*, story paper, drawing materials

Activity:

Read *Quick as a Cricket* to the children. Have them brainstorm adjectives which describe what they're like as the child did in the story. Help them think of animals which share those descriptive adjectives. Tell the children to choose 6 adjectives which best describe themselves. Using the story as the model, have the children make their own books about themselves.

Extensions:

- For further work in developing analogies use *Hippogrif Feathers* and *Strange and Familiar*.
- Look for analogies in school activities, e.g. children in a lunch room are like ants at a picnic. Stuffing peanut butter in celery and putting raisins along the top makes a snack like ants on a log.
- Do a family book describing family members.

Stanish, B. (1981). *Hippogriff Feathers*. Carthage, IL: Good Apple Pub.
Gordon and Poze. (1972). *Strange and Familiar*. Cambridge, MA: S.E.S. Assoc.
Wood, Audrey. (1982). *Quick as a cricket*. Singapore: Child's Play (International) Ltd.

LANGUAGE ARTS
Class Activity

Letter Lovers

Language Arts Objective: letter writing
Creativity Objective: originality
Materials Needed: plain paper, print-making materials, e.g., stamps, ink pads, stickers, block prints, potato prints, envelopes

Activity:

Show the children different kinds of stationery. If possible, have someone from your local stationery shop visit and show a variety of stock.

Have the children design and print 10 sheets of stationery and envelopes. Then, introduce the proper form for a friendly letter. Have the children choose someone to whom they want to write and have them write to that person. Teach them how to address the envelope and send the letters.

Extensions:

- Begin a pen pal club with another class or school.
- Join the Artifact Exchange (Contact: Scott Johnson for additional information.).
- Develop a greeting card center.

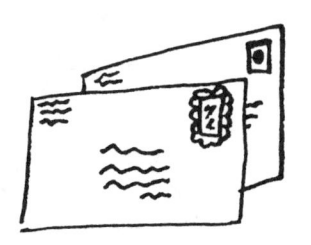

LANGUAGE ARTS
Class Activity

Pass The Bag

Language Arts Objective: understanding of the parts of a story
Creativity Objective: fluency, flexibility
Materials Needed: 1 lunch bag for every 4 children, 5 small items for each bag, e.g., eraser, handkerchief, ball, bandaid, doll's shoe, baseball card. Each bag should contain different objects.

Activity:

Have the children work in groups of four. Give each a bag and have them write a story using the objects in their bags. Collect the stories when the groups are through but do not share the stories yet.

Go through the activity another day giving each group a different bag this time. Continue repeating the activity until each group has written about each bag.

Then, compare and contrast the groups' stories that go with each bag. Point out the fluency of ideas and the children's flexibility in using objects.

Extensions:

- Have the children create story bags and trade them with three other children.
- After reading a book, have the children create a bag to go with the story. Have the child use the items in the bag to give a book review to the class.
- Create a display for your school by showing the items in the bags and the children's stories they generated.

LANGUAGE ARTS
Independent Activity

Photo-biography

You will get better at: organizing and categorizing information in a creative way.
You will need: paper, pencils, pictures, old magazines, paste, photographs of you

Activity:

Tell the story of your life. Use pictures and photographs to illustrate the story of you. You can cut out photographs and paste them on pictures or create other combinations on your own! Be sure to include the special events, places and people in your life. You can also have a futures section showing what you would like your future to be like.

When you've finished, you might want to bind your photo-biography. Ask an adult to help you with this part.

Tips:

- Ask people who know you to tell you the stories they remember about you growing up.
- Look at your baby book, family pictures and video for ideas.

How did I do?

	Yes	No
I showed the different ages of my life well.	___	___
Anyone who reads this photo-biography will know a lot about me.	___	___
I organized my book well.	___	___

LANGUAGE ARTS
Independent Activity

Artistic Readers

You will get better at: finding main ideas, designing posters.
You will need: a good book, poster paper, paints or markers

Activity:

After reading a good book, do you usually tell your friends so they can read it, too? This time, show them instead of telling them. Design a poster that will make people want to read a book you like.

To make a good poster remember:

1. Use a few important words (not a lot of extra words).

2. Use colors that show up well from a distance.

3. Use shapes or pictures to attract eyes to them.

4. Pick 1 or 2 main ideas (not everything you know) about the book.

Design a poster on your book to convince others to read it, too.

Tips:

- Look at posters you like. How do they use color, words, pictures?
- Think about what you want people to know about the book.
- Remember to give enough information about the book so someone can figure out what book you've read.

How did I do?

	Yes	No
I am happy with my poster.	___	___
There is enough information about the book on my poster.	___	___
People notice my poster.	___	___

LANGUAGE ARTS
Independent Activity

To Pop or Not to Pop Book

You will get better at: thinking of ideas.
You will need: construction paper, 15 paper balloons, string, paste, markers

Activity:

Together with 2 friends, think of many ways to pop a balloon. Try to think of ways no one else will think of. Select 15 ideas to put in a book.

Each of you in your group is in charge of 5 ideas. Design a page for each idea. Paste a paper balloon on the sheet and draw your idea around it. Remember to add words.

Make a cover and staple or bind the book together. Donate the book to your library for other children to read.

Tip:

Print neatly and draw brightly-colored pictures.

How did I do?

	Yes	No
We thought of many ideas.	___	___
Some of the ideas were funny.	___	___
Some of the ideas could really happen.	___	___
Other people liked the book.	___	___

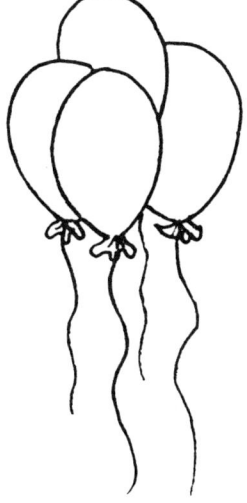

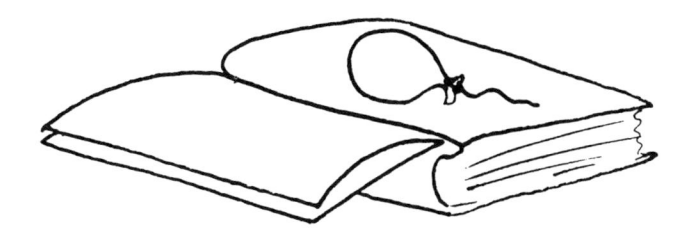

LANGUAGE ARTS
Independent Activity

Mother Goose, Where are You?

You will get better at: rewriting things in your own words.

You will need: a Mother Goose book, paper, and pens

Activity:

Can you recognize this story?

> An egg man
> Downed himself on something very high.
> The oval individual rolled off.
> Every riding animal owned by the ruler
> And every man working for him
> Were not able to fix the oval character.

You guessed it! It's Humpty Dumpty.

Now, choose another rhyme and rewrite it, changing all the words to different words that mean the same thing. See if your friends can guess the rhyme.

Tip:

Use a dictionary or a thesaurus to help you think of other words.

How did I do?

	Yes	No
I changed all the main words ("a", "an", "the", "and" don't count).	___	___
My friends guessed the rhyme.	___	___

LANGUAGE ARTS
Independent Activity

Mobile Mystery

You will get better at: describing and retelling stories.
You will need: a copy of a favorite book, construction paper, glue, markers, tape, string

Activity:

List all the characters in your book. Try to think of what the characters look like, what they like to do, things they did in the story. Take a piece of drawing paper for each character. Draw pictures of the character on his or her page. Put the name of the character and a few words to describe him or her on each page. Attach the pictures to string and make a mobile.

Have others guess what book you read.

Tips:

- Have an adult help you with the knots and the balancing.
- Small pages will not curl as much as big pages.

How did I do?

	Yes	No
I remembered all the characters.	___	___
Others could guess the book by looking at my mobile.	___	___

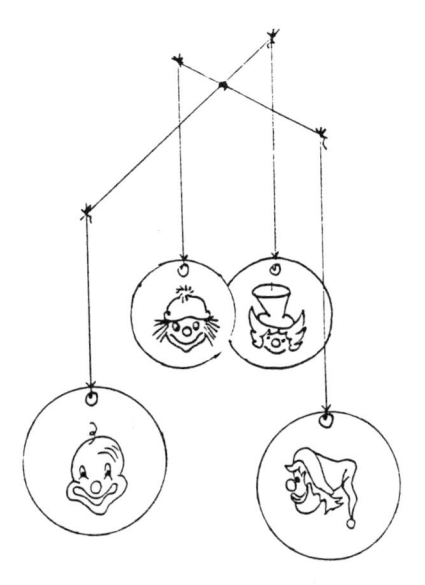

LANGUAGE ARTS
Independent Activity

Mood Molding

You will get better at: understanding what words mean, sculpting.
You will need: the word list (below), pictionary or dictionary, clay, camera

Word List: jubilant, thin, silly, shy, fatigued, angry, cool, weird, mysterious, dizzy, morose, jolly, furious, lazy, bored, fat

Activity:

Choose a word from the list and find out what it means. Create something out of clay to illustrate the meaning. You can make it look real or make-believe.

When you are happy with your clay sculpture, take a picture of it for a class pictionary.

Tip:

If you are not sure of the meaning of the word after you have looked it up in the dictionary, ask your teacher or parent to explain it to you.

How did I do?

	Yes	No
I know what my word means.	___	___
My friends can guess what my word means by looking at my sculpture.	___	___

Creative Project For the Language Arts Buff

Title: Talk of the Town

Lucky you! You have just won the opportunity to produce a five-minute radio show for an educational radio station. You are in charge. You decide what news, information, or topics you want to tell your listeners. Start thinking!

Idea: You will create a five-minute radio show about an important topic.

Get Ready...

- Listen to public radio, and watch educational TV shows for ideas to talk about.

- Ask your pals what they might like to hear on radio besides music and sports.

Get Set...

- You will need a topic (You will have to write a script).

- You will need a tape recorder, microphone, and a blank tape.

- You will need a timer.

Go!

The Plan:

Do First:
1. Make a list of topics you think kids should know about.
2. Start the one that is most important to you or the most interesting.

Then:
1. Make a web to help you see all the parts you may want to talk about. (See web example at right.)
2. Research each part that you want to talk about. (Hint: Ask an expert; check with your librarian; watch a film or filmstrip about the topic.)
3. Decide on the best order to present your topic, and number sections on web.

Quality Control:
☐ Have you used your 5 minutes well?
☐ Is the recording clear? Not too fast? not too slow?
☐ Is your voice loud enough?
☐ Is your talk interesting?

Web Sample:

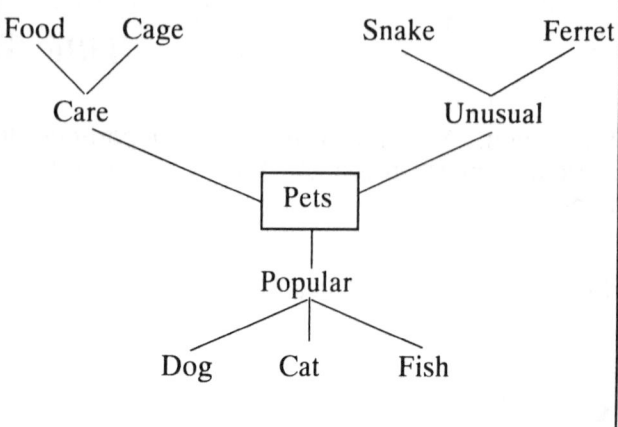

Food   Cage   Snake   Ferret
    Care   Unusual
              Pets
            Popular
       Dog   Cat   Fish

Finally:
1. Prepare your broadcast. The following outline may help you write your script:

    A. To Begin:
    1) Tell an interesting fact to begin your talk.
    2) Tell people what they will learn from your radio braodcast.

    B. In the Middle:
    1) Begin with the 1st section on your web. Tell what you know about that part.
    2) Do this for each part.

    C. The End:
    1) Remind your audience what the topic was one last time.
    2) Tell them the 2 most important things that you hope they learned and will remember about your talk.

2. Practice giving your talk into the tape recorder. Limit it to 5 minutes.
3. Listen to your talk. You may add sound effects or music if you wish.

If you are happy with your results, play the tape for your class.

Creative Project For the Language Arts Buff

Title: Extra, Extra! Read all about it!

Do you get tired of your family's asking, "What did you do in school today?" Here's one way to solve that problem. Write your own class news. It will answer your family's questions about what you've been doing, and it can also tell them important things that will be coming soon. You're the editor, so you decide.

Idea: Design your own class news.

Get Ready...

- Do you like to write?

- Do you like to talk, interview other people?

- Do you like to draw?

- Do you like to read the newspaper?

Get Set...

- Decide who can help you find out what is going on in your class and school.

- Get materials: paper, pencils or pens, notebook (so you won't lose ideas.)

- Practice with a computer (if you have one), typewriter or neat printing with a dark pen.

- Work with your teacher to decide:
    - where you will keep your materials.
    - where you will work on your project.
    - when you will have time for this project.

Go!

129

The Plan:

Do First:

1. Gather newsletters for ideas on how to organize your news. (Hint: Check with school librarian, principal, parents.)
2. Brainstorm a list of events, things you want to tell about in your class news. (Tips: class trips, birthdays, favorite library books, special projects)
3. Star the events, things that are most interesting. You can include these in your class news.
4. Think of a name for your newsletter.

Then:

1. Make sure you have all the information you need for your starred events. Hint: You may need to find out more information. So:
   1. Interview someone: take good notes.
   2. Do a survey.
   3. Be a good observer.
2. Decide how you will tell about each of your starred events. (Hint: You may decide to use a picture, chart, story, cartoon, etc.) Use your creativity.

Finally:

1. NOTE: If you're lucky, your school has a computer program for newsletters — ask your teacher. If not, you can use a computer, typewriter, or neat printing to complete your project.
2. Look at your newsletter collection again to help you select a layout. Type or print your stories one column wide. Then cut and paste up your class news.

Quality Control:

☐ Does your newsletter look good?
☐ Are the words and names spelled correctly?
☐ Is the information accurate?

(Hint: Find someone to be your proofreader.)

If you have completed the quality control check, you are ready for printing your copies and sharing your class news. Congratulations!

Creative Project For the Language Arts Buff

Title: Believe it or not!

Do you think that Paul Bunyan's ox, Babe, was really blue and that...?
Tall tales like this begin with the truth but grow and grow until it's hard to tell what's true and what's not true. People like to exaggerate to make a story more exciting or daring. Tall tales do that. Do you think you can invent a tall tale?

Idea: Write your own tall tale based on something you've done or what someone you know has done.

Get Ready...

- Read some tall tales for samples.

- Can you tell what's being exaggerated?

Get Set...

- You need paper and pen, or computer.

- You need a hero or heroine.

Go!

The Plan:

Do First:
1. Decide who this story will be about.
2. Make a list of things this person does.
3. Star the things you can exaggerate to make the story more exciting.

Then:
1. Make a storyboard of the adventure that your hero/heroine could really have.
2. Using the pictures in your storyboard, write the story.

Finally:
1. Change your story by exaggerating details or the parts that will turn your story into a tall tale!
2. Choose the best part of your story to illustrate. Then, draw illustrations to go with your story.

Quality Control:

☐ Do you have a hero/heroine?
☐ Is there a true story underneath your tall tale?
☐ Do you have some exaggerated — bigger than life — parts?
☐ Can other people read your story? (Hint: Is your handwriting neat? Did you spell everything correctly? Did you use capital letters and punctuation marks?)
☐ Do your illustrations show the most exciting parts of your story?

If you'd like, now is the time to share your story with others!

Creative Project For the Language Arts Buff

Title: Pic Pick

When you hear a story, do you ever close your eyes and try to imagine what the people and places in the story look like? Hers's your chance to put your imagination to work. All you need is a camera and a good short story or a poem or a song.

Idea: Make a slide and tape show of a favorite story, poem, or song.

Get Ready...

- Think about stories, poems, or songs that you like. Make a list of those that tickle your imagination, one that make you see lots of pictures in your mind's eye.

Get Set...

- You will need a storyboard planning sheet.

- You will need a camera that uses slide film.

- You will need a roll of slide film.

- You will need a copy of your story, poem, or song that you can cut and paste onto your planning sheet.

Go!

The Plan:

Do First:
1. Think of pictures that you could photograph that will go with your story, poem, or song.
2. Draw these ideas on your storyboard.
3. Cut up the part of the story or poem or song that matches the picture.

Then:
1. Have an adult show you how to use the camera.
2. Take photographs of your picture ideas (remember to use slide film).
3. Remember to do a title picture and credits. Your teacher will give you ideas how to do this.
4. Get your film developed.

Finally:
1. Arrange the slides in the order of the story, song or poem.
2. Put the slide in the slide tray and view them using a slide projector to make sure the slides are in the right order and not inserted backwards or upside down. Your teacher can help.
3. Put tape in the tape recorder.
4. Go back to the first slide and start the tape recorder. Tell the part of the story or poem that goes with each slide. If you chose a song, sing or record the song on the tape. Show the slides to match the parts of the song. Your storyboard will help you to remember which slide goes with which part of the story, poem, or song.

Quality Control:

☐ Are your pictures clear?
☐ Is the tape easy to understand?
☐ Do you have enough pictures to go with the tape?
☐ Do the tape and pictures go together well?

If you answered "yes" to each, then it's showtime!

Creative Project For the Language Buff

Title: In my Family

Is your family like any other family in the whole wide world? Probably not! Every family has some special things about it — things that they do in their own special way. These things are called family customs.

Idea: You can make a book about the things that make your family special.

Get Ready...

- Read *Ashanti to Zulu.**
- Think about the special things your family does.
- Ask grandparents, parents, aunts or uncles about family customs.

Get Set...

- You will need notecards, construction paper, markers, paste, the book *Ashanti to Zulu.*

Aliki. (1976). *Ashanti to Zulu.* NY: Dial Press.

Go!

The Plan:

Do First:
1. Pick six customs that your family observes. List these in your book.
2. Jot down on your notecards the information you can gather about these customs.

HINT: Does your family have birthday parties for family members? Does someone bake a special cake? Is there a special candle they light each year?

Then:
1. Collect artifacts (pictures, special decorations, or things used for your special events).
2. Decide what order you want to put your events in.
3. Write a paragraph explaining each family custom.

Finally:
1. You will model your book after *Ashanti to Zulu*. For each event you will have one page where you must draw your information and paste on an object like the candle that goes on the cake.
2. Paste your paragraph at the bottom to tell about the custom.
3. Draw a border around the page like the illustrator did in *Ashanti to Zulu*.
4. Make a nice cover for your book.

Quality Control:

☐ Did you organize your pages in a nice way?
☐ Does each page have a border, artifacts, drawing and text?

Isn't you family special?

Part IV
Other Opportunities To Enhance Creativity.

Creative people do things.

There are many ways to incorporate creativity into the school day. In this section we will discuss forming a think tank, creative use of bulletin boards, centers and special moments.

Think Tanks

One way is to view children as problem solvers. Let them be your "think tank."
As you consider your classroom, where are the places for you to:

— provide materials which can be used to "create" solutions to special problems you pose to the children?

— display a hands-on activity for any child to do in a spare moment?

— work with small groups of children in a problem-solving activity?

To develop these options, try the following:

Using a shelf, an extra desk, or a table, provide a "Create Your Own" area. Present a problem and some materials which could be used in solving the problem. Changing them every week or two will keep the young problem solvers coming back.

PROBLEM	MATERIALS
Create a new Community Helper Uniform	Paper, crayons, pictures of fire fighters, police officers, doctors, mail carriers, veterinarians, etc.
Develop a name and masthead for our town's newspaper	Paper, pens, examples of newspaper mastheads
Create a school mascot	Paper, crayons
Create your own cartoon character	Pens, cartoon frames on a ditto
Design a "favorite saying" board for a good friend	4" x 4" wooden plaques, alphabet noodles, glue, paints, brushes

Bulletin Boards

Do you have a spare bulletin board begging for a new idea? Take another opportunity for creativity by using the bulletin board.

Bulletin boards can provide a hands-on activity for children when the top provides the invitation and the bottom offers the activity well within reach.

INVITATION	ACTIVITY
• _____ = 5	Using computer cards (or paper strips) and a marker, children develop the equations that equal five. (100 - 95, 10/2, 6 - 1, 1 + 2 + 2)
• RED ROUND (Venn diagram with car, apple, ball)	Using 3" x 3" squares of paper, children draw or print words that can be categorized in the Venn diagram.
• "I Can Fit in a Breadbox"	Using 3" x 3" squares of paper, children draw pictures or print words that answer the invitation.
• FINISH ME! (squiggle)	Using a squiggle, children finish the drawing.
• AND FROM THE WINDOW I SAW... (window drawing)	Using dittoes with a window on them, children show what they saw (or would like to see).

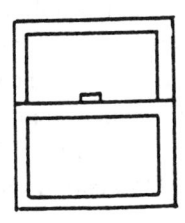

Centers

Exciting learning centers have strong appeal to children. They can be process or content oriented so the skills of creativity training and the content of a curriculum area may be combined. To make a center successful its activities should:

1. Be varied, allowing different ways of expression.
2. Be open-ended, encouraging many answers.
3. Allow hypothesizing and hypothesis testing.
4. Encourage both individual and small group projects.
5. Allow for mucking about.

Centers can provide many options for encouraging creativity and enriching the classroom activities. To make them successful the children must have time to use them The center activities must be changed when interest begins to lessen. The children will need to know what is in the centers. One way to inform them is to develop advertising campaigns for new center ideas. We developed a Coming Attractions bulletin board. This bulletin board announced the changes in the centers. A sequence for a coming attraction might be: (Monday) You'd better begin flexing finger exercises. (Tuesday) Get your dictionary ready. (Wednesday) Watch for Mood Molding. (Thursday) Class meeting to introduce the activities. We have found that the children will want to introduce their own activities or develop the advertising campaigns for the centers.

Invention Center

Materials: batteries, small motors, pulleys, prisms, color wheels, wheels, magnets, straws, string, wire, doorbells, and assorted "junk"

The children were encouraged to muck about with the materials, combine them, and invent something. As they learned about simple forms of energy and began applying what they learned, they showed some amazing ingenuity.

A group of third graders were working with the wheeled vehicles: a roller skate, toy truck, and a tricycle wheel. They wondered which of the three would travel the farthest. They decided to devise an experiment to find out. The first problem they encountered was the influence of the initial push on the vehicle. To standardize the release, they decided to build a ramp. The ramp would allow them simply to release the vehicle. After several tests, each trial was carefully measured and recorded. They concluded that the tricycle wheel would travel the farthest. It kept rolling to the wall. They wondered how far the wheel would go. Their curiosity led them to move the experiment to the hall. The wheel rolled right out the front door! The escaped wheel gave them the idea of writing a story about the wheel that would not stop. After writing the story they decided to make it into an animated film.

This series of activities reinforced skills in math (measuring, graphing), science (hypothesizing, balance, energy), language arts (story writing), reading comprehension (sequencing), and art (film). Most important, the skills were relevant to the children's interests.

The children used the invention center to solve other problems in curriculum areas. Second graders established an utopian community for warm fuzzies. They used the center to create inventions for the fuzzies.

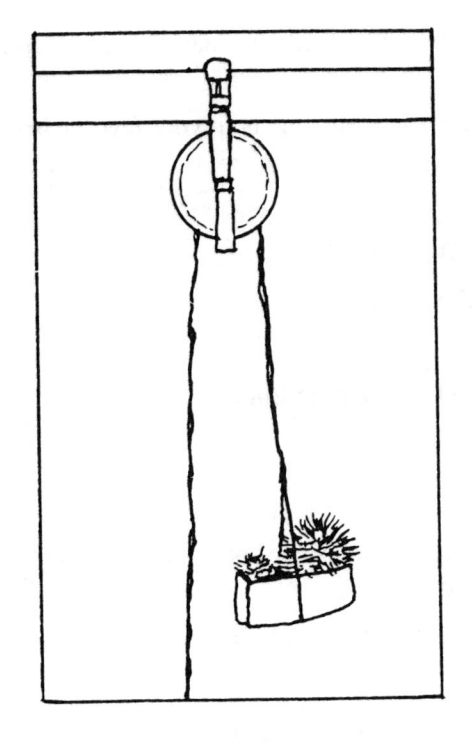

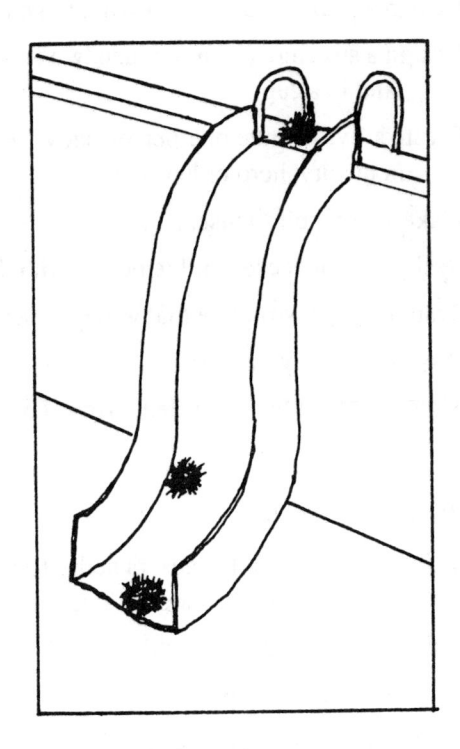

ELEVATOR FOR FUZZIES   SLIDE FOR FUZZIES

DISCO FUZZIES

During this unit the warm fuzzies were invaded by the cold pricklies. The children had to decide how to get rid of the invaders. A child who rarely contributed anything to class projects went to the invention center and worked hours inventing an electro-magnet disguised as an oil tank. He placed a thumb tack in each cold prickly. During the next class discussion he announced his plan. Since the cold pricklies used oil for fuel, they would approach the oil tank unaware that it was now a magnet. Once within range they would be absorbed. He demonstrated the effect to the delight of his classmates.

Ideas for young inventors

Design a peanut cracker that will not smash the peanut.

Design a structure (no more than two feet high) that will allow a marble to travel five feet and land in a cup.

Create a five-minute one-person show, with costume, to tell about your favorite book, person in history, hero or heroine.

Make a better birdhouse.

Design a book jacket for the book entitled, "Our Class."

Design a paper structure that will be a pencil holder.

Make a better fly swatter.

Write a cartoon book entitled, "How To Care For Your Pet Bug."

Animation Center

Materials: 3" x 5" note pads, pencils, 16mm leader film, story board paper, movie camera that will take 400 speed film, and tripod

The possibilities are endless for this kind of a center, but try these for starters:

Have the children make flip books.

A flip book is a series of pictures in which the object is changed slightly from page to page. The 3 x 5 note pads allow the child to flip through the action when the drawing is finished without having the pages fly all over the room. It's better to begin with a single object such as a rolling ball, a flying bird, or an erupting volcano. Once the children understand the skill, they can develop more complicated actions. For a science assignment, a child could make a flip book showing the life cycle of a butterfly. A follow-up activity might be to change the last part of that flip book to make people laugh. The cocoon could unveil an ice-cream-eating gnome. For a math activity, a child could make a flip book about a triangle meeting a circle. Once the children are proficient at making flip books, they can move on to film.

Have the children make animated film.

It's really not difficult. The following two sources are excellent. They give clear, manageable instructions for designing animated films.

Laybourne, K. (1979). *Animation Book*. Crown Publishers.

Andersen, Y. (1985). *Make Your Own Animated Movies*. Boston: Little, Brown & Co.

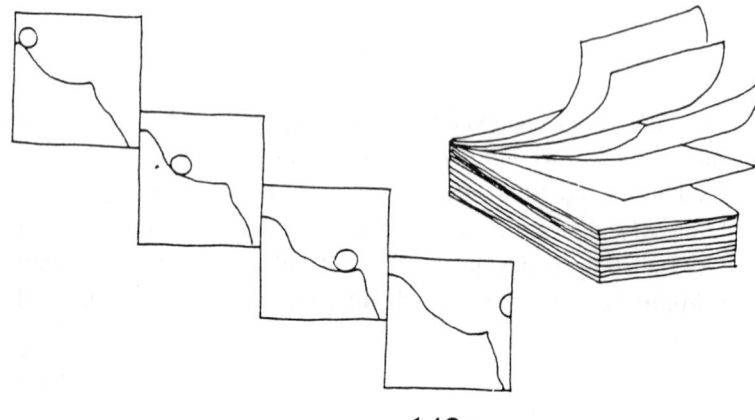

Creative Arts Center

Materials: pencils, crayons, dictionary, thesaurus, typewriter, clay, construction paper, instamatic camera

The following are examples of themes that we developed for this center. We changed the themes on a regular basis. The length of time can vary depending on the age of the children, the interest in a particular theme, and the availability of materials.

CREATIVE COLORING: Complex designs are available in the center.

1. Make the design futuristic. Give it a title and a history suitable for a museum description.
2. Take two of the same designs. Color one with warm colors and the other with cold colors. Describe the difference in mood.
3. Do anything to the design except color it.

WARM FUZZIES
1. Read the book *The Original Fairytale.**
2. Make a warm fuzzy out of wool, and list ten ways to use it.
3. Invent a greeting card for the new holiday—Warm Fuzzy Day.
4. Write a poem explaining what it feels like to be a warm fuzzy.

MENU MANIA
1. Draw four wacky hamburgers, and give them names.
2. Invent a sandwich. Write a letter to the patent office to patent your idea.
3. Invent magical foods that will turn people into space creatures. Name each food, and draw the consequence of eating it.

* Steiner, T. (1976). *The Original Fairytale*. Sacremento, CA: Jalmar Press.

More Center Ideas

Here are five center ideas to help establish environments which foster creativity:

1. Publishing House

    a. Design a pop-up book.

    Have several old pop-up books donated so that the children can examine the paper engineering or use *How to Make Pop-Ups.* *

    b. Design magazine covers for your favorite magazines.

2. Futuristic Fashions

    a. Use Barbie dolls, paper dolls, or a drawing board. Have fabrics, crayons, etc. around. Pick a variety of planets, future dates, and future wants and design fashions accordingly. Have the students name their favorite free-time activity and decide how it will be different in the year 2001. Have them design an outfit to wear that accentuates the differences.

    b. Have the children compare fashions from history and make some modifications to update them for the future. For example, Star Wars costumes strongly resemble costumes of the Middle Ages.

3. Artifact Antics

    Bring in pieces of objects, such as a shower nozzle, a roller from a window shade, a can of Pepsi, a bicycle wheel, plastic file case, etc. Hide one or two a day in a box of sand. Have the class select teams of young archeologists. Let them pretend that they had dug these items up, and have them answer these open-ended questions:

    What is it? Where did it come from? Why is it here?

    What will you do with it? What else can you do with it? (Hint: great place to brainstorm more ideas) The class can decide which team of archeologists has the most original answers. They can also decide which group elaborated the best.

4. Greeting Card Center

    a. Create a holiday. Circle it on the calendar. Create a line of greeting cards to commemorate the day. One class started a Warm Fuzzy Day. Everyone was to attend to the good traits of others, and compliment them. Warm Fuzzy cards were designed and given out. It was such a success that it became a school tradition.

    b. Have a birthday committee to design cards for peers, and present them on their birthdays.

    c. Young writers and young artists can combine their efforts for a line of cards that may be given as gifts or sold.

Irvine, J. (1985) *How to Make Pop-Ups.* NY: Morrow Jr. Books.

Special Moments

There are certain times in a school year or day that lend themselves particularly well to creative thinking. One of these cases is the class party. We told the children that the Christmas Party was going to be futuristic. The children began to brainstorm what a Christmas Party would be like in the year 2180. Ideas flowed fast and furiously. From a list of thirty ideas, several were chosen for elaboration:

1. Refreshments: space cookies, moon punch, intergalactic straws
2. Games: pin the moon on Saturn, anti-gravity jump, laser beam tag
3. Grab Bag Gifts: space creature puppets, nuclear Christmas balls, comic book — *Prehistoric Adventures of Robot Man*

The class divided into committees to elaborate on each of the areas. Each member of the refreshment committee baked space cookies. The cookies ranged from a gigantic robot to four small, round, multi-colored circles. When asked what the circles were, the student replied, "food pills." The four circles represented a four-course dinner of the future. The moon punch was a concoction of various fruit juices in a bowl decorated as a moon. The other committees developed their ideas equally well.

Much time is spent traveling to and from special activities during the day. One second grade teacher tired of forever telling her students to keep their line straight and to be quiet. She began giving them instructions for creative movement. Her class of twenty-four could be seen as a double-dozen-a-ped, the March wind, and the abominable snowman and his followers as they moved in and out of the building.

Another marvelous moment is the first snowfall. The chances of keeping the children's attention during this event are slim so you may as well take the opportunity and spring into action. Divide the class into groups. Have them create a production entitled, "The First Snow." One group could choreograph a dance, another could write a poem, one could interview a snowflake as to its mission on earth, and another could design a bulletin board.

If you can set the stage for creativity by being fluent, flexible, original, and elaborate, it is likely that your enthusiasm will be contagious, and your example followed.

Five More Minutes Worth Seizing

1. Lost tooth
    a. Design a certificate.
    b. Write a story of the tooth's whereabouts.
    c. Draw a picture of a substitute tooth that grew in its place.

2. Full Moon
    a. List 10 magic events caused by a full moon.
    b. Invent a special kind of gnome or fairy species that dances in the light of the full moon. Make a mural of the event.
    c. Transform the surface of the moon into a fantastic playground.

3. Report card day
    a. Design a report card for your best friend, teacher, parents, pet, or favorite toy.
    b. Write an editorial about why we need or don't need report cards.
    c. Design a report card for children attending school in the years 84 B.C., 1492, and 2861.

4. First day back after Christmas Vacation
    a. Take a survey of how many toys received as holiday toys are already broken.
    b. Design a travel poster advertising where Santa may not be vacationing.
    c. Design and create a calendar for the New Year, dedicating each month to a favorite story-book character. Plan activities during that month to honor that character. For instance, May could be Alice in Wonderland month. A tea party could be planned. A Mad Hatter's day could require a hat-designing contest.

5. Birth of a sibling — "Annie has a sister."
    a. Create a badge to honor Annie.
    b. Write a poem to commemorate this day in history for Annie's family.
    c. Draw a family portrait of how the family will look in ten years.

Closing Thought

The whole art of teaching is only the art of awakening the natural curiosity of young minds for the purpose of satisfying it afterwards.

Anatole France

Bibliography

Callahan, C. M. (1978). *Developing creativity in the gifted and talented.* Reston, VA: Council For Exceptional Children.

Darcy, J. (1989). *Fundamentals of creative thinking.* Lexington, MA: D.C. Heath & Company.

Davis, G. (1989). *Creativity is forever.* Dubuque, IA: Kendall Hunt.

Davis, G. (1987). "What to teach when you teach creativity." *GCT,* Jan., pp. 7–10.

Feldhusen, J.F. and Treffinger, D.J. (1977). *Creative thinking and problem solving in gifted education.* Dubuque, IA: Kendall Hunt.

Getzels, J.W. and Jackson, P.W. (1962). *Creativity and intelligence.* NY: Wiley and Sons.

Houtz, J.C., Rosenfield, S., and Tetenbaum, T. (1978). "Creative thinking in gifted elementary school children." *Gifted Child Quarterly, 22,* pp. 513–19.

MacKinnon, D.W. (1978). *In search of human effectiveness: Identifying and developing creativity.* Buffalo, NY: Creative Education Foundation.

Parnes, S.T. (1977). "CPSI: The general system." *Journal of Creative Behavior, 8,* pp. 1–11.

Renzulli, J.S., Owen, S., and Callahan, C.M. (1974). "Fluency, flexibility, and originality as a function of group size." *Journal of Creative Behavior, 8,* pp. 107–13.

Stanish, B. (1981). *Hippogriff feathers.* Carthage, IL: Good Apple.

Sternberg, R.S. (1988). *The nature of creativity: Contemporary psychological perspectives.* NY: Cambridge Univ. Press.

Strickland, M. (1974). "I was a wrong answer kid." *Journal of Creative Behavior, 8,* pp. 153-56.

Torrance, E.P. (1962). *Guiding creative talent.* Englewood Cliffs, NJ: Prentice Hall.